MW00463630

FIRST PRIORITY

A Father's Journey in Raising

World Champion Surfer Carissa Moore

Copyright © 2017 Christopher Moore

All rights reserved.

Cover Design: Christopher Moore

christopher.moore85@gmail.com

Cover Photo: © Grant Ellis

Back Cover Photo: © Christopher Moore

Red Bull's marks are registered trademarks
of Red Bull GmbH.

ISBN: 9781520782768

To Cayla
For your love and understanding.
For being the best daughter I could possibly ask for.

Foreword
by Carissa Moore

My dad believes in me. Knowing that he believes in me, sometimes more than I believe in myself, has been extremely empowering. He knows my ability better than anyone and encouraged me to do things I never thought possible.

In the very beginning, surfing with dad was purely fun. We'd go tandem surfing at Waikiki several times a week. I remember it being a bit of a struggle at times to pull me away from the television but once we got in the water the rest of the world melted away and it was just dad and I. Our surfs were usually short, afterwards we'd play in the sand and swim in the shallows which made the experience even better. It was so special to have time just for us.

When I realized that surfing was my passion and that I wanted to win a world title, dad was ready. He saw my potential and believed that it was possible. I remember him telling me, "If this is what you want, I will help you. It's going to be a lot of hard work. There will be tears and you will have to make sacrifices but it will be a lot of fun." He was right.

I quickly learned what dad meant. With my parent's divorce and school, time for surfing was limited. Dad stressed that if I wanted to be the best, I had to work harder and smarter than everyone else. He would wake me up at five am to surf before school and was waiting for me as soon as the bell rang to take me back to the beach. I was hungry, tired and often grumpy but he knew what it took. I went to sleepovers and had to leave early when the waves were good. My dad saw it as an opportunity to get a step ahead. It was such a bummer at the time but now I understand how important those sacrifices were. Dad's dedication and experiences as a competitive swimmer shaped me into the athlete I am today.

My dad is a thinker. He loves a game and relishes in a challenge. After taking last place in the Sunset Gidget Pro trials in 2008, my dad decided it was time to think outside the box and change things up. In 2009, he proposed that Pancho Sullivan and Myles Padaca should coach me at Sunset in preparation for the contest. One of the things I admire and appreciate about my dad is that he doesn't have a big ego. He realized he couldn't teach me everything so he found the right people to do so. Pancho and Myles were the perfect fit for me as I ended up advancing through the trials to win my first World Championship Tour event at seventeen.

Coming from a non-surfing background, Dad and I had to learn to do things our own way. There were no limitations or expectations on how it should go so he was never afraid to take chances. Although I was oblivious at the time, Dad had a plan when he entered me into boy's events and professional women's events at a young age. He believed in my potential and saw the benefits of stepping outside my comfort zone. He has encouraged me to never sell myself short, to give it everything I've got and not to care what anyone else thinks.

Our journey has been imperfectly perfect. We've yelled at each other and have gotten frustrated. At times, he's made me cry and I've made him lose his mind. We don't have it all figured out, but through this journey, we've come a long way in handling stressful situations and conflicts. We know when to take a break and figure things out after we calm down. Today, Dad is more aware of the appropriate times to push me and I try not to take his constructive criticism so negatively.

Overall, our good times have far outweighed our difficult moments. The greatest gift my dad has given me is his time. We've traveled the world together. He's spent countless hours driving me to and from the beach, watching my practices, giving me advice, filming, organizing trips, talking to sponsors, traveling and enduring jet lag while toting heavy board bags. Material things will fade but the memories we have made together, the time spent listening, laughing and learning is what will last a lifetime.

It's been an incredible journey so far. Thanks, dad, for everything. I wouldn't be where I am today without you.

Preface

We're in the middle of a supermarket on the North Shore of Oahu. Carissa is crying. She wants to quit. It's pretty much all my fault. She just lost a surf contest, and despite my initial efforts to hold in my disappointment, my compassion transforms into something much less respectable. An interrogation ensues. I question her tactics. I highlight her mistakes. My frustration is obvious. In return, my daughter says the one thing I never wanted to hear.

"Dad, I don't like surfing anymore. I'm done."

"Fine, quit," I retorted.

That all-too-familiar condescending parental note hung in the air of the produce aisle, floating somewhere between the green bananas and the imported apples.

We had just finished the Haleiwa Menehune Surfing Championships, one of the largest surfing contests for kids in the state of Hawaii, and it hadn't gone as we had planned. Early every fall, kids from all over the state gather with their families to share the sun and surf at Haleiwa Ali'i Beach Park. For the young surfers—often referred to as groms, or keikis, or, in the case of this contest, menehunes—the surf was small and playful, the water clear and warm. There was a slow and gentle wave breaking near the shore. Regardless of the size of the swell on the open ocean, given its sheltered location it's a perfect spot for beginners and young children, and overall it had been an easy, friendly day on the North Shore.

As usual, the annual contest is well attended, and the beach park was littered with picnics and pop-up tents. This year, event organizers had to turn away kids who entered late. For as much aloha as there is in the air, there's a competitive edge underlying it all. By the later rounds, the contest had transformed from a fun beginner event to something more serious. Part of the young competitors' angst comes from wanting to win not only the contest, but also the splendor of goodies on display. New surfboards, watches, backpacks, leashes, and other swag are there, just waiting to be taken home by some stoked kid. For parents, it can be equally as trying for a whole different set of reasons.

I had entered Carissa in the Girls 7–9 division. She had been surfing well all day, easily advancing through her heats. Come the final, I was nervous, yet extremely confident that my daughter would crush her pint-sized foes. The heat started well enough. Carissa caught a good wave and made the most of it. As she paddled back out, I thought to myself, "One more good one and you've got this." Victory was hers. I could taste it.

Almost as soon as she got back out to the takeoff zone and sat up on her board, a beautiful three-foot set feathered out the back. As if by magic, the biggest and best wave I had seen all day was steaming straight at my daughter.

"Yeah! This one, Carissa! Paddle! Paddle! Go! Go! Go!"

The chorus echoed silently through my skull. Wary of being the obnoxious parent, I kept my anxious thoughts private. But, to my surprise, Carissa continued to sit, seemingly uninterested in what was coming her way. How was she not seeing this?

My internal dialogue screamed, "This one, Carissa! This one! Move! C'mon, paddle! Now!"

My best efforts to psychically channel commands to her failed, and the wave passed underneath her as she continued gazing innocently out to sea. For Little League parents, it has to be the equivalent of watching their child pick daisies in left field as a fly ball soars overhead. I stood up and threw my hands in the air. And finally, my words audibly screamed out.

"What are you doooing?!"

Carissa's main rival didn't sit and watch the wave pass by. She spun around, paddled, and surfed the wave all the way to shore—and to victory.

As Carissa exited the water, I met her on the shoreline and began my interrogation: "Didn't you see that wave? Why didn't you paddle for it? That was the best wave of the day!"

I'm not exactly sure what Carissa said—it was fifteen years ago, and I wasn't taking notes—but it probably went something like this:

"Dad, I just caught a wave and paddled back out. The other girls were waiting longer."

Looking back, it simply didn't matter what she said. She could have explained to me that she saw a sea turtle or got a bout of the hiccups. She was eight years old, and an eight-year-old shouldn't have to put so much emphasis on winning.

At the time, I couldn't let it go. I continued to "coach her" on how to better control the lineup and not give her competitors any chances whatsoever. Dejected, Carissa silently walked up the beach and took a shower. I hastily stuffed our belongings into the car. As soon as the awards were over, we practically peeled out of the parking lot. Carissa held herself together for as long as she could, but by the time we pulled over to the market to pick up a few snacks for our long drive back home, she was bawling.

Then, again, my internal monologue kicked in: "Chris Moore, you're a fricking bonehead!"

Immediately I realized I had lost sense of my direction. I had lost the stoke and joy that I intended to create for her. Because of my actions, she was ready to walk away from something that had started as pure, unadulterated fun.

Nobody prepared me for any of this. Before we left the hospital after Carissa was born, the doctor didn't tell me that she was going to be a freak athlete, nor did he hand me a how-to book on how to raise her. Now, years removed from the scene at Foodland, I look back and think about what a remarkable challenge we've overcome together.

For the past twenty-two years, for better or for worse, I've been riding the wave as a father and coach, and I wouldn't want it any other way. As I write this, Carissa has already won two professional surfing world titles and I couldn't be more proud of the young woman she's become. Right now it's the World Championship Tour (WCT) off-season and she's spending her time in Haiti distributing water filters to families in need for a non-profit organization called Waves for Water. As a father, that makes me as proud as any competitive accomplishment.

In just a few weeks, the 2015 World Surf League (WSL) WCT season will begin. Last year Carissa stumbled down the home stretch and missed out on another world title, so with the wound still fresh she's trying to reset. In our off-season conversations she wanted me to refine her approach in an effort to put a serious campaign together to win another title. She asked me to travel with her and help as needed throughout the year. Of course I said yes. We've made it work in the past and I am confident there's still a lot in the tank when it comes to competitive success.

The following is an around-the-world glimpse inside my daughter's world-title ambitions and the role I played in helping her accomplish them.

As a parent and a coach, sometimes I get it right, sometimes I don't. But at the end of the day it's still just a dad and his little girl crazy enough to chase dreams.

1

We're in the middle of a supermarket in Tweed Heads, Australia. Carissa is filling our cart with basic provisions: eggs, bread, fruit, yogurt. Our grocery list, much like our relationship, has evolved through the years. When we first started coming here, a decade ago, novel goodies like Tim Tams and bags of pancakes would find their way to the checkout counter. Now, with years on the road to lean on, we opt for the healthy stuff. Well, except for the Tim Tams. I distract Carissa long enough to slip a pack into our shopping cart, just underneath the Nutri-Grain Cereal Bars.

We arrive back to our rented flat, where our living room looks like a small surf shop that's been hit by a hurricane. Surfboards and boxes of surf gear are strewn about. Carissa has twelve boards lying on the sofa; six new boards were waiting for her when she got here and she had brought another six from Hawaii. An array of wetsuits, bikinis, leashes, traction pads and surfboard wax sits in piles on the floor. The clutter is chaotic, but manageable; we'll have it sorted well before her first-round heat that's slated for tomorrow.

We're in town for the Roxy Pro Gold Coast, the opening event of the 2015 World Surf League Championship Tour. This will be Carissa's sixth year. Sometimes it feels like one long marathon. This career of hers—traveling the globe, surfing, and getting paid for it—is the best job I can think of. But it's also a dizzying combination of an exciting occupation and a tremendously difficult one. The reality of chasing waves and world titles is that there is an infinite number of ocean and weather conditions to contend with. Simply put, if Carissa figures out these variables and then performs better than her rivals, she stays on the seventeen-spot roster and chases world titles; if she doesn't, she falls off. Fortunately, for the past six years Carissa's been on the positive side of this equation. Here in Australia, getting ready for another lap around the globe, Carissa and I ease into our time-tested routine.

A small swell is currently pulsing on the Gold Coast, affectionately referred to as "the Goldie" by surfers. There's enough surf at Snapper Rocks for the WSL to call the contest on, and like that our campaign is underway. Carissa gets off on a good foot. In small, playful surf, she grinds out a win.

"I feel good," confides Carissa back at our flat. "My boards felt good, I wasn't too nervous. What did you think?"

I tell her it's a good start to the season, but I don't elaborate much past that. My role is complicated, as I'm not here only as her father, but also as her coach. Part of my job description is to give her an impartial assessment of her performance after heats. I've learned over the years that the best thing I can do in situations like this is keep things simple and ride the positive momentum. I've put my foot in my mouth more than a few times; I know better than to get into the nitty-gritty and risk overanalyzing her performance, especially after the first round of the first event of the season.

The next day, the ocean goes flat. The contest is forced to go on hold, which means one thing: waiting. Specifically, waiting for waves. In order for the contest to be held, there has to be surf. To help insure that the surfers have something to ride, each stop on the schedule is typically given a ten-day waiting period in which to run. An event can wrap up within two to three days if surf conditions are prime, but that's seldom the case. Officials monitor the surf forecast in the event window and optimize which days are best to run the show. If Mother Nature is fickle, the contest is pushed into a holding pattern. This waiting period translates into an excessive amount of downtime, and when you're trying to maintain a competitive edge, that can be a killer. For me, who's signed on to help support and coach my daughter, it's bothersome. I don't like the waiting around.

One down day turns into another, then another, and another. On our fifth "lay day," as they're often referred to, Carissa makes plans to go sightseeing with friends.

Carissa knows my response, but is gracious enough to still ask, "Hey, I'm going to the wildlife reserve. Want to come?"

I've seen enough koala bears and kangaroos in such excursions during previous contests on the Gold Coast, so I decide to hang back. Alone in the apartment, it's certainly a beautiful day. The sun is shining. The ocean is tranquil. It is a pleasant scene, perfect for a vacation, perhaps, but for me it's akin to beachside purgatory. I should relax and soak it all in, but I'm not here to do that. I'm here to support my daughter and I want to get down to business.

I stare at the half dozen clean, white surfboards that have been moved and stacked on the carpet and begin to think about which ones will bring some magic to Carissa's next-round performance. Finding a "magic board" is not nearly as easy as one would think. By now Carissa should have had a chance to test all these different boards out, but being that the surf is so small, there's nothing to ride, and subsequently I have nothing to do. It is moments like these, little quiet windows of time, that I let myself drift back.

It started over twenty years ago, just before Carissa was born. I'd taken my wife, Carol, to see Bruce Brown's *The Endless Summer II* in the theater. I vividly remember watching in awe as a five-year-old boy ripped the waves on the North Shore of Oahu, just a thirty-five-minute drive from my house. Since he was so small, his dad would push him into the incoming swells. With his dad's help, he wasn't just going straight in the whitewater; he was standing up, bottom-turning, and zigzagging across the face. I'd never imagined a kid that age could possibly surf that well. I'd have to say he was Carissa's first surfing influence.

Watching those moments in the film inspired me to see if I could turn Carissa into a little water bug too. Without a doubt, watching those images of a little five-year-old surfing head-high waves was the moment when lightning struck. Carissa never really had a choice after that. In the early weeks and months of her life I placed her ever so gingerly on a surfboard. It started in the living room. Eventually she graduated to our backyard pool.

Though there was never a grand plan of raising Carissa and her younger sister, Cayla, to become world champions, I did have motivation. I taught my girls to surf because I thought it was a wonderful pastime I could give to them—and with the selfish hope that they would never want to live anywhere else but Hawaii. I reasoned that since Hawaii has great surf and warm tropical weather year round, they'd never move away when they grew up.

I spent hours teaching Carissa to swim. We'd spend afternoons at the beach paddling around in the shallows. We'd discover the sea life below and enjoyed our time together in the water. It was never work. Our adventures were primarily centered on us just being together. We spent time in the ocean learning and playing. We developed routines where I would flip her into the air and she'd land feet first into the water. She would lounge on my back or chest as I swam. We spent countless hours building sand castles. The ocean was always a place of fun, an escape, somewhere we could spend quality time together. Those early years were just playing in the ocean, like kids have done on the South Shore for centuries.

When she was two years old we started tandem surfing together in Waikiki. After awhile we developed our own set of tricks. She would stand on my shoulders or prop herself in a sitting position on the nose of the board, howling like some crazed animal. We received a fair amount of amused, if not perplexed, looks from nearby surfers. I was sensitive not to push our activity too long, ensuring our sessions came to a sweet close whenever she got too cold or just wanted to go in. Those years teaching and playing in the rollers at Queens, while forever engrained in my memory, today seem like an entirely different life.

2

There's a lot of nuance when it comes to competing on the World Tour. The main reason I am still along for the ride is because I help Carissa sort out what she needs to focus on at each event. I'm here to wade through all of the variables so she can focus on her job: winning heats and, ultimately, world titles.

The cornerstone of our preparations is Carissa's understanding of the waves she will be surfing. Each location has its own unique set of characteristics, and knowing how a wave will break is key. Some break quickly, others with an exceptional amount of power, while others gently peel down well-sculpted points. There's really no replacing firsthand experience at a spot, which means logging as much water time as possible wherever we are. Waves are constantly changing. From hour to hour, a surf break can be completely different, and that's where I come in. I work on ways to gather information and give advice on how to take advantage of what the ocean's offering up.

Every year, the Roxy Pro is held at Snapper Rocks, which was recently named a World Surfing Preserve. Where the contest is held is actually part of a much longer wave known as the Superbank. Snapper Rocks is the first section of the mile-long, world-renowned sand-bottom point that peels into Rainbow Bay. Like all locations in the surfing world, the Superbank has its own unique characteristics, and in this case the wave is actually enhanced by man's hand. A perfectly tapered sand bottom is created when sand is dredged and then pumped from the mouth of the nearby Tweed River to the top of the point at

Snapper Rocks. The sand is then swept down the point by ocean currents. As it settles, it creates the ideal bottom contour for waves to break across with ruler-edged precision. When all the elements come together, the wave can offer a ridiculously long ride with some of the best barrels on the planet. But there's a catch. The Superbank is rarely super. The winds, tides, and weather systems that create swell have to align for the break to work just right. And when it turns on, it seems like everybody in Australia shows up to partake.

With all of these uncontrollable components bouncing in play, I do my best to stay on top of weather and swell forecasts. Staying up to date on storm models, forecast charts and ocean data has become more than just a passing hobby over the years. I can be downright obsessive about it all because so much of our lives is dictated by what's happening in the atmosphere. One day it's four-foot, glassy, and beautiful; the next, the ocean's turned angry. The more I understand these rhythms and weather patterns, the more likely I will be able to help guide Carissa to the best waves. When it comes to winning world titles, taking some of the guesswork out of it is a huge advantage. My number-one topic of conversation with contest directors, team managers, surfers, and parents centers around swell forecasts, primarily where and when the next heats will be run. The cocktail of swell forecasts and heat predictions usually leaves me with a serious headache.

My challenge is to shield Carissa from any of my aforementioned feelings and opinions and just give her the facts: swell direction, wave size, wind direction, and heat times. After all, I'm trying to alleviate any anxiety she may have, not add to it. I do my best to make sure she is ready to surf when the time comes. I take care of coaching duties and try to keep her calm and balanced, in addition to ensuring she is fed, rested, and happy.

It's been about fifteen years since Carissa's life as a

competitive surfer—and, subsequently, my life as a surf coach—began. Every year, we navigate that delicate balance of coach and father. At times my role gets confused and conversations turn to arguments. Sometimes they're legitimate. Sometimes they're not.

Carissa reads a lot into what I say, and I'm the first to admit that in many conversations I could have articulated something more eloquently. But it goes both ways. I can praise her through most of a conversation and then be critical of one aspect of her surfing and she'll focus on the critique (regardless of the number of compliments handed out prior) and overthink its significance. Sometimes there's no real critique; it's her interpretation of what I said that might turn into something that bothers her.

Our relationship has evolved dramatically over the years. In the past, if one of us was bothered by something, we usually would spend way more time than was necessary dealing with the irrational side of the issue. My initial reaction has always been to challenge her—which may or may not have always been the best approach. Though we continue to improve with our communication, we still have our moments, especially around events, as contest time brings out Carissa's more emotional side.

On one of the down days at the Roxy Pro, Carissa walks up the beach after her morning surf and asks, "So what did you think?"

"I liked it," I say. "You did a good job handling the crowd and you managed to catch some of the better waves. Though the waves were small and there weren't many sections that allowed you to open up, when you got on a good one I thought you performed well."

"Yeah, there were some slow sections, but I really liked the board," answers Carissa. "What do you think?"

"Yeah, I liked the board too, especially on the good sections. I'm not sure about the junk sections, though; it looks like it's bogging a bit," I say. "You know who I thought had a good board for the flatter sections? Steph [Gilmore]. Her board seemed to carry through the flat sections here a bit better."

"So you're saying that Steph is more ready and has better boards than me?" quickly answers Carissa.

"No, I'm not saying that. I'm saying that her boards look better in flatter sections, that's all," I repeat as calmly as I can while trying not to show any hint of defensiveness. I know where this is heading, and I immediately brace myself for the fallout.

Carissa's frustration is obvious. She quickens her pace to walk ahead of me, another sign that she is not happy with the conversation. I feel like I need to say something to remedy the situation. So I do. And I immediately make matters worse.

"Would you rather have me not tell you the truth?" I ask, and in those words my frustration cracks through my attempts of remaining calm. This scenario has played out countless times. It's part of our regular back and forth, and we know all too well which buttons to push.

"Dad, why are you freaking out?" says Carissa, storming off farther ahead.

The benefit of having so many conversations like this is that by now we know how to remedy them. At the apartment we collectively take deep breaths and regroup. The conversation settles down. We realize we are getting worked up about something silly. She knows her surfboard shaper, Californian Matt Biolos, is in town and that he is able to shape and glass boards for her almost immediately. We decide to give him a call and see if he could make her some last-minute boards in case she has to surf in poor conditions. The value of a reliable surfboard shaper cannot be overstated.

Matt, who is a surfboard supplier to a number of pros on Tour as well as a father, tells Carissa not to worry and that he'll get on it right away. He understands her predicament perfectly. He gets to work and in less than twenty-four hours Carissa has three new boards to try. Options always seem to put her mind at ease.

Later on Carissa and I discuss our disagreement. We talk more rationally and work through things. I clarify what I meant to say—that Steph's surfboards don't look better than Carissa's in the good sections, and that's where it's going to matter most. And for her part in it, Carissa understands there's really nothing all that off about her equipment. As successful as she has become, and as much as she wants me to travel with her to contests, we still get into these tiffs from time to time.

We both realize it's all part of the journey. Just the same, it's important to figure it out, solve it, move on, and not let it get the better of us. And for the most part our relationship remains unfazed. After all, we're both doing something we really love to do. It should be fun—except for the losing, of course. But that's another story.

3

Midway through the event holding period, a tropical cyclone appears on the forecast models near Fiji. There's a good chance of epic surf hitting the area. The problem is that the swell is expected to arrive a couple of days late and the contest directors are forced to apply for a permit extension through the Coolangatta City Council, which has everyone looking at the very real possibility of even more waiting. It's hard on everyone's nerves. It's also incredibly expensive because everyone, from the surfers to the judges to the webcast staff, has to change their travel arrangements.

Twenty-four hours later, it becomes a reality. Officials add two more days to the waiting period. Thirteen lay days in a row and finally we will determine an event champion. It's officially the longest contest holding period ever.

Indicative of a charged ocean, an electric salt mist hangs in the gray dawn air. The new swell arrives as forecasted. The subtropical Tweed River breeze blows sticky. The sun hasn't risen yet. The streets are dark. It's still quiet save a few WSL workers buzzing around the contest site. There's no question the show will begin promptly at 8 a.m. In our apartment, the tension is palpable.

Sharing passing glances as we go about our respective breakfast routines, Carissa and I both know what's in store. We talk briefly about what boards to bring down to the contest area. Carissa knows what she wants to ride and I don't want to confuse things by questioning her decisions. It's time for her to focus, to channel her motivation.

As I choke down my cup of coffee I am overcome by an upwelling of anxiousness. I do my best to strike a stoic pose and my apprehension gets internalized. My own psyche is of little consequence. I force myself to exude an air of calm amongst my building angst. Whether it's something as simple as preparing a backup board for her or grabbing an extra tube of sunscreen, I shuffle around busying myself with handling minor tasks and eliminating distractions. I'm here to offer constructive feedback when asked, but my biggest chore is just to stay out of the way.

Not being in control is not my forte. I do everything I can to keep the handbrake on my natural inclinations. It has taken time to figure out. All of the struggles and stress we encounter, it's part of the game. Winning a world title is a series of battles, and we know that going into every season. The challenge is to put all the pieces together over the course of the year. There are good times and bad times; sometimes it feels like we're ad-libbing the whole thing, but the goal is always to put a world title trophy on the mantel at the end of the year.

I tell myself she's put in the work. She's prepared. Everything is going to be just fine. I would do anything for my daughter, but what I cannot do is paddle out and perform for her. That she has to do on her own. She's alone out there in the water. No matter what I do, nothing changes that. So here I am, a complete wreck. I have to endure all the nerves, but have no hand in the eventual outcome. It's been like this since her first surf contest.

For this contest I've arranged some specialty coaching. In the past it has proven very successful to employ a surfer who lives in the area and knows the break to help impart some wisdom and knowledge. In this instance Carissa is paired up with former world champion and Australian icon Wayne "Rabbit" Bartholomew. One of the real revolutionaries of the sport, he played a large role in ushering in "pro" surfing in the late '70s and has been surfing Snapper Rocks his entire life. He's an obvious choice to give Carissa pointers on where to sit and what waves to look for. It's good for her headspace to have somebody like that to listen to.

"You need to make sure you're picking the right waves that hit the sandbank and grow," explains Rabbit as he points out to Carissa visual cues to look for as the waves wind down the point.

Getting a wave that provides the opportunity to perform at a high level is harder than it sounds. The waves at Snapper can be deceiving as they come in. Waves that initially look good fizzle out into deep water. Small waves often grow in size and get better as they progress down the sandbar. Catching the right wave is important because it allows a surfer to perform more maneuvers, increasing their opportunity to obtain a higher score. Finding these waves is key, and in a half-hour heat there may be only a handful of these waves that come through. For Carissa to win, she has to be on them.

Rabbit goes over last-minute details before Carissa's quarterfinal heat. I'm around too, but as heat time approaches I make it a point to fade into the background. Surfing heats is by now old hat for her; I know that giving her space is the best thing I can do. I take a less-is-more approach, since in most cases too much meddling causes only confusion. I am confident in her ability. It's up to her to rise to the occasion.

Carissa advances to the semifinals and then to the finals. Despite being behind early in both rounds, she keeps her nerve. She selects the right waves and performs accordingly. She looks strong and confident, and when she's like this it makes my job—which at this point includes not throwing up from all of the stress—so much easier.

4

Carissa is up against defending event champion and hometown hero Stephanie Gilmore in the finals—the same girl we were fussing about just a few days ago. Steph isn't just another female on tour. She is *the girl*. She's the current star of women's surfing and the only woman on Tour other than Carissa with a world title—six, actually— to her name.

She's easily the toughest draw in the contest. In addition to being the dominant performer on Tour for the past eight years, she knows Snapper Rocks like the back of her hand. She lives across the street. If there is a home court in surfing, this is hers. Yet despite being at a distinct disadvantage surfing against Steph at her home break, this is the match-up Carissa wants. In the minutes leading up to her final, Carissa is quietly confident and focused. She is ready. She wants this. I can feel it.

The final starts. In thirty-five minutes, we'll have a champion. Steph grabs the first good wave, linking a number of stylish, well-executed turns together. The judges give her an eight-point score. It gives her an early lead.

A few minutes later, Carissa finds a "grower." It's just what Rabbit told her to track down out there. She tears into each turn with authority. She rips off a series of five huge carves linked together by fluid, effortless transitions. She kicks out emphatically. She knows that she's nailed a ride. The judges drop a 9.40 out of a possible 10 points.

World-tour heats are decided by adding together the top two wave scores each surfer gets in the allotted time, and Carissa already has a near-perfect score in her tally.

There's a good chance that with one more high-scoring wave she'll be able clinch the win. There's ample time remaining and she knows she just has to be patient and wait for another wave that allows her to perform. The judges are looking for commitment and degree of difficulty in the maneuvers she performs, in addition to the speed, power, and flow with which she executes them. Whatever wave comes her way must allow her to weave all these elements together in one dynamic ride.

Against the hometown favorite with serious wave knowledge, she's going to have to contain her nerves. And I'm going to have to figure out how to contain mine. Carissa has twenty-six minutes left on the clock to wait for the wave that will allow her the opportunity to win the contest. A lot goes through one's head in that amount of time.

Staring out to sea for a minute, I get lost in another memory: Waikiki, Carissa, age five. After I'd prepared her to deal with the ocean, my daughter was finally able to swim for minutes at a time and dive under waves on her own. I felt she was comfortable enough in the water and was ready to surf on her own. For this effort she earned herself a yellow-and-blue soft-top surfboard. She was thrilled.

My goal was to make surfing as enjoyable as possible. To make the long paddle out a little easier, on most days she would lie down on her surfboard and hold onto my ankle as I escorted her out to the lineup. I used a similar technique launching her into waves. She would hold onto my foot as I paddled her into position. As the wave caught up to us, I would bend my knee and scoot her up beside me, then at the right moment I'd reach back, grab her foot and give her a final push. She'd shoot forward and have plenty of time to get to her feet before the wave broke.

While most kids were trying to figure it out by

themselves in the whitewater, Carissa was surfing on the clean face of the wave. With so much time spent on the open face, it was easy for her to practice her turns—not unlike the five-year-old I'd seen surfing on the silver screen just a few years earlier. As we got better with our system, we began to catch more and more waves. Occasionally, I'd hear wry comments: "Hey, when can I get my push?" Looking back, it probably drove other surfers crazy, but the peanut gallery never fazed us.

For Carissa it all seemed so natural. Her ability to stay in the prime part of the wave, her stance, her grace— even at five—seemed clear. She was going to be a great surfer. And though I felt so sure of her ability, I also realized that I had to navigate my desire to get her to where I thought she could go. I was completely aware of my ability to mess the situation up.

One day I asked a friend to take photos from the beach. I managed to push her into a beautiful wave that walled up and peeled perfectly across. Carissa stood up and began shooting across the open, blue face, but as it started to speed up she hesitated and mistimed the section. Instead of having a fast down-the-line ride and getting "the shot," she got swallowed up by the whitewater and wiped out. She was held under and came up shaken and teary.

My response was ridiculous: "What happened? You could've made that!"

I was too focused on my friend getting a good photo to notice that my daughter was upset. She needed me to console her, but instead I did the opposite—I let her know I was disappointed. Looking back, I wonder why I ever acted like that. But then again, maybe if I'd been too soft none of this would have happened. It's one of those tough parenting dilemmas that sometimes not even hindsight can make sense of.

5

With nine minutes remaining on the clock, I'm snapped out of my reminiscing by a solid set lining up behind the rock at Snapper. It's time to perform. Carissa has to surf fast, show effortless improvisation and put emotion and power into her turns. The judges won't buy a safe or tentative performance. She has to want it. She paddles. She stands up. She proceeds down the line with unwavering conviction.

She hammers five critical turns and kicks out. The judges drop another nine-point score for the effort. Carissa has an insurmountable lead. Minutes later, it's over. She's won the first event of the year. The moment is hers.

Friends rush to "chair" her up the podium. Tradition dictates that Carissa's feet are not to touch the sand from the water's edge to the top of the podium as her friends carry, or chair, her up the beach. A lot of flag-waving and revelry ensures, then the hugs and high-fives. Photographs and interviews soon follow. Then the trophies and champagne—and a fat check for sixty thousand dollars.

I watch from a distance, glowing, tremendously proud. As soon as the awards presentation concludes, I collect her belongings and head back to the apartment. I am content, again, with taking care of the little things—carrying boards, washing laundry, packing for our flight home.

Chores complete, I head over to the Coolangatta Surf Club, where I find Carissa partaking in the longstanding celebratory tradition known as "skulling" a drink. Three-time world champ and local icon Mick Fanning commands the pub's attention while Steph, whom Carissa has just beaten, hands her a Red Bull and vodka. A raucous victory song erupts. Carissa's task is to take down the drink in one big gulp.

Now, Carissa doesn't have an expansive drinking history. Sipping a mojito on a rare occasion is, as far as I know, the extent of it. So pounding a drink in front of the roaring crowd doesn't exactly come naturally to her. After sheepishly asking what exactly she is supposed to do, being the resourceful person she is and knowing that pounding a whole drink in one go could end only in disaster, she improvises. Halfway through her attempt, she alters course and dumps the remaining contents over her head. The bar erupts. I have to smile and laugh at the whole scene. This year's already promising to be quite a ride.

6

The morning after her win, we're back on a plane heading home to Oahu. Carissa's not the vagabond surfer-type; she gets homesick, and frankly, so do I. Professional surfing keeps her on the road for at least six months of the year and it's a challenge to balance normalcy. Instead of spending a few weeks in Australia between Tour stops, she opts to return home to visit family, tend to her house and spend time with her boyfriend and high school sweetheart, Luke Untermann. I think it's great that she balances her time and priorities the way she does.

Back home, we slip into our routines. I get caught up on work, though through the years my workload has significantly decreased. Running my own graphic design business, it's hard to keep a client base being away as much as I am. Carissa gets back to working with her trainer and surfing her favorite local breaks. We have two weeks until we head back Down Under and we make the most of it.

Over the next two months she has four World Tour contests with very little time in between. Because of this I keep a lighthearted mood during her practices. Regardless, the excitement and pressure of being back on top of the rankings creeps into her head. I'm used to this; she's been on top before and has certainly done her share of worrying and stressing. I think most of her concerns are far from valid, but I do my best to quell her fears. Sometimes our conversations are as hilarious as they are ridiculous.

"Dad, do you think I'm doing enough? I just don't know. I'm feeling a little off," Carissa tells me after coming in from a surf.

With her statement, I immediately know what she's looking for. She wants me to give her the reassurance that she's on track. I tell her she looks great and remind her that she struggles with her emotions at times when she's in a good position. It's been like that her whole life.

"I'm not sure about how I looked at Snapper," she continues. "I thought I looked slow and wasn't turning that hard."

"You won the event. Who are you comparing yourself to? Filipe Toledo?" I say half jokingly.

Filipe, an energetic, next-level kid from Brazil, won the men's event at Snapper Rocks and at the moment appears to be surfing at a level a notch above everyone.

"Yes," she says in all seriousness.

I laugh. I don't know why I am surprised by this statement. Carissa's tendency to compare herself with male surfers comes from her early experiences in surfing. From a young age I was telling her she was as good as the boys. I was the one entering her into a boys' division when the opportunity presented itself. I made it a personal challenge to help Carissa keep up with her male peers for as long as possible. I watched what the better boys were doing in the water and worked with Carissa to replicate it.

We embraced this challenge quite early—in fact, almost at the very beginning of her contest career. The Haleiwa Menehune contest was the first contest I ever entered Carissa in. The first year, when Carissa was five, I entered her in the kokua division, where parents could assist their kids by pushing them into waves near shore. This division was purely introductory, as there were no winners or losers. It gave the kids a chance to surf together and get the feeling of surfing in a contest—and winning! All the children who competed came away with a trophy and some goodies provided by surf companies and North Shore businesses. We had a great time. We didn't need to be serious. It was just for fun.

It was the next year that things got more serious, especially for me. I wanted to see if Carissa could win against the boys. I figured she had a good chance. She was starting to surf a lot more and I hadn't seen any other kids her age surfing as well as her on the South Shore. In the weeks leading up to the contest, our lighthearted after-school surfs took on more focus. I worked with her so she could catch her own waves and we even made a few trips to Haleiwa to practice.

On the day of the contest, I made sure we got to the beach early so we could jump in the water and catch a few waves before the heats began. After her warm-up, we made our way over to the heat sheets pinned on a nearby palm tree. Carissa was one of twelve entrants in the 6 and Under division, with both boys and girls. Even at her early age, I was excited for her to compete. I assured her she'd do great and have fun, but inside I wanted her to win. I found myself not only getting competitive, but also nervous, mainly because her success or failure was now completely out of my control.

She surfed in the first of two six-person heats. It was a success. She advanced easily into the final. In the second qualifying heat I watched a bleached-blond kid surf effortlessly to victory. He looked even better than my daughter and I realized we might fall short of ultimate domination in the 6 and Under division.

Before the final we talked heat strategy, which went something like this:

"OK, you ready? Paddle out about as far as those kids are over there. Then, when a good wave comes, stand up, head this way, and do some turns!"

She paddled out and did just that. She surfed well, but the blond-haired kid surfed better. At the awards ceremony later that afternoon, Carissa walked up to receive her runner-up trophy. All told, it was not a bad outing for her. The kid who went on to win is named John John

Florence, presently considered by many to be the best male surfer on the planet.

It seems to be in Carissa's DNA to not be satisfied. It takes different forms and it can manifest unexpectedly, sometimes when things are looking up and there's no rational reason. I can understand the behavior because it's part of my genetic makeup too. I exhibit a lot of the same thought patterns myself. Eventually she realizes that against the women she looked pretty damn good. She knows she competed well and pushed her surfing. Carissa settles herself down and sets her sights on the next leg of her journey.

7

Ping-ponging back across the Pacific, we're back in Australia. This time we're in Torquay, Victoria, for the historic Rip Curl Pro at Bells Beach. Founded in 1973, it's the oldest contest on Tour; it's hard not to be struck by the nostalgia of the place. I imagine it's like playing baseball at Fenway Park or Wrigley Field. We can feel the history here. It's inspiring.

On the Gold Coast, the weather was hot and the water was warm, but here at Bells we have to contend with a different set of elements. The air and water are decidedly colder—typically around sixty degrees Fahrenheit—and the ocean is considerably more moody. The weather and waves come storming up from the Southern Ocean with all the power and fury you'd expect. For Carissa, a tropical girl at heart, the cold presents a challenge.

I've had to contend with a girl from Hawaii competing in chilly water for years and it's taken some work to get used to. Most of the year Carissa surfs in not much more than a bikini and maybe a lycra vest. But logging time in California, Europe, and here in Australia, she's had to get used to pulling on a full body wetsuit. Designing flexibility and comfort in these neoprene second skins has been a top priority for years, and the wetsuit manufacturers have advanced the technology considerably, but that doesn't mean the suits aren't still somewhat constricting and inhibitive. In her pre-teens, when Carissa first started having to wear wetsuits regularly, she felt awkward and confined. Finding a wetsuit that fit properly was a challenge. But each year her wetsuits have gotten lighter and fit better. Presently, her favorite wetsuits come from Japan. Because the rubber the manufacturer uses is very stretchy and supple, she's able to have better feel and range of motion when going in and out of maneuvers.

For the Bells contest Carissa is greeted with a box of new, bright, orange and black wetsuits. In the warm-ups leading up to the contest she seems to be wearing the new suits well. The big problem is that her feet still get cold. In the past, on days when she's surfing an early heat, she's complained about not being able to feel her feet and respond the way she would like when up and riding. It's a common issue for many surfers, but my daughter seems to be especially sensitive in this area. Her feet lose feeling and feel heavy—not a good combination when she's trying to surf at her best.

At last year's event I found myself microwaving heating pads and wrapping them around her feet in an effort to bring circulation back. It paid off: her warm feet carried her to a second consecutive Bells title. A year later and she's sporting a secret weapon: heated shoes. It's a perk of her Hurley/Nike sponsorship. When learning that one of their athletes has to deal with cold feet, the biggest shoe company in the world comes to the rescue. The end result: heated boots that she can plug into any wall outlet. It took most of the year to get the highly customized footwear, but before the event a package containing a comfortable and stylish pair of black boots with heated toe warmers arrived on her doorstep. The boots may not win the contest for her, but they do help her feel a little more comfortable. And if Carissa's feeling good and happy before her heat, and her feet are warm, then that's a good thing.

8

As it seems is so often the case, the day before the contest is scheduled to start the surf is beautifully shaped. The weather's sunny, the winds calm, and for this part of the world it's a pretty nice day. The break at Bells Beach consistently pulses with long, sculpted, head-high walls winding through the bay. Ironically, great surf can prove to be as frustrating at times as no surf at all. That's the way it goes at many of the world-tour stops. When the surf is good, word spreads quickly and a lineup full of the planet's best surfers can make for a crowded—and cutthroat—surf session.

On this day, it seems all the competitors on the Tour—men and women—want a piece of the action. Catching one of these beauties is about as easy as trying to catch a gazelle on the open plain. With so many great surfers in the water, everyone is constantly trying to out-position one another, often paddling deeper into the lineup in an effort to gain right of way. Catching waves becomes frustrating; I think it might be as frustrating for me to watch as it is for her to surf. There's solace in knowing that she's not alone. Most of her peers come in feeling the same way.

Though the conditions are pristine at the moment, the weather is forecast to turn. We are looking at a below-average surf forecast for the event's holding period. But regardless of the conditions, the break on most days is a great canvas for Carissa. The underwater reef shelf offers predictable takeoff zones and a variety of peeling right-hand waves during high and low tides that allow for hard, carving, forehand turns. Having won the contest for two years running now, when the conditions are favorable out there Carissa's tough to beat.

I settle Carissa's nerves by helping her realize that imperfect Bells can be an amazing canvas for her as well. Her first-round heat is testament to this, as she scores two excellent rides in the wild and windblown surf for the heat win.

She's surfing well and her feet have been toasty. Not surprisingly, her new heated footwear is the hot topic around town. Some of the other competitors are envious and inquire about how they can score a pair. Too bad these babies are custom.

Of course, all good things must come to an end.

"Uh, dad, my feet aren't getting very warm," Carissa says after putting them on and realizing they were no longer heating her toes.

"What do you mean they're not working?" I retorted, a bit befuddled that the boots weren't working—and on finals day, too.

"My feet aren't warming up," she says matter-of-factly.

Looking back at it, I should have figured it out a few days prior when Carissa and fellow Hawaiian Tour surfer Alessa Quizon were screaming frantically in our apartment.

"Dad, get over here! The blender's on fire!" I heard Carissa yelling.

I found them in the kitchen panicking as their food processor was smoking and shooting sparks from its tiny engine. I had to laugh as two of the best surfers in the world were freaking out over a burning food processor…that was sitting only inches from the kitchen sink. As far as the girls were concerned, the house was engulfed in a raging inferno. I simply unplugged the food processor, turned on the faucet and pushed it into the sink.

The girls, as well as myself, didn't realize that

electrical amperages in Australia are different than back home, so instead of liquefying fruits and vegetables into a delicious smoothie, the appliance almost set our living quarters ablaze. I surmise that Carissa's boots have suffered a similar fate. In the end, we find ourselves resorting to last year's routine of heating beanbags in the microwave in the competitors' area at the contest site.

Boots or not, Carissa's surfing well and aces her early quarterfinal to advance into the semis. As the draw plays out, she finds herself matched up against one of her most formidable foes, Sally Fitzgibbons. Sally's a tough competitor no matter what the venue. She's gritty and plays the game with savvy and determination. She hates to lose and never gives up. When Carissa and Sally are in a heat together, it's full on and it usually goes down to the wire. The two have surfed against each other seventeen times, with Sally having an edge when it comes to wins with nine. Moreover, the past four Bells trophies have been split between the two.

As their semifinal kicks off, a fierce battle for priority plays out. Both girls, wanting to get the first good wave of the heat, try their best to out-paddle and outsmart the other by getting closer to the breaking part of the wave and thus earning the right to catch the wave without being penalized. It's a critical moment in the early stages of the heat.

It was part of our strategy: before the heat started, I'd told Carissa to aggressively battle for position. I'm sure Sally paddled out with a similar intent. For the first ten minutes the girls aggressively jockey for position, each doing their best to maneuver for the right to catch that precious first wave. It's a hard ten minutes for me to watch.

I'm trying to maintain a portrait of composure from my vantage point on the iconic Bells stairway that leads from the cliff down to the sand, but it certainly isn't easy, especially with a WSL camera zeroed in on me. I wish I wasn't part of the show, so I do my best to be as stone faced and unexciting as possible with the hopes that the cameras will move on to something more interesting. Watching heats and internally managing my angst is tricky business, especially when there are times when I want to throw my hands in the air in exasperation.

Time ticks away and in these first ten minutes it's all defense. Neither girl catches a wave. The head judge resets the clock in accordance with the WSL rules; heats are restarted in the event that neither surfer catches a wave in the first ten minutes.

"Great!" I mumble under my breath. "Ten more minutes of added stress to my day."

Almost immediately after the restart, the waves turn on. Both girls start off with average scores, but midway through the heat Carissa paddles into a well-shaped wall and links a few powerful rail turns for a nine-point ride. Sally counters with a seven-point ride to keep herself within reach.

As the heat winds down, Carissa controls priority. A set approaches the lineup. She keeps Sally off the last wave with any scoring potential. She's into the final.

9

In the final, Carissa meets Stephanie Gilmore for a rematch of their Snapper Rocks clash. The heat starts slowly. Once the girls hit the water, they have to sit out in the lineup, cold feet and all, for fifteen minutes as the broadcast team presents their pre-finals show. I'm beside myself. Will Carissa be able to turn properly with numb feet by the time she finally stands up on her board?

The silver lining is that at this event, cold feet during the final is the biggest concern I've had to deal with. Everything else has gone remarkably smoothly. During most events there's an issue or two that keeps life for Carissa, and myself, a little off balance. However, during the Rip Curl Pro things are running smoothly. Seeing that she is firing on all cylinders and that her mental outlook is positive, I keep things light. I occasionally inquire how she is feeling, but more than anything I do my best to stay out of her way.

Hoping to give my daughter an advantage, for Bells I called upon a local surfer, Cahill Bell-Warren, to help her with her surfing and heat strategy. With Cahill in her corner, my job before her heats is to give her some encouragement and then disappear.

"You've been here, you've done this, you know this place like the back of your hand," says Cahill, reaffirming the messaging I've been using all week. "The bowl is working right now, so line yourself up with the stairs," he continues. "The waves will come; just be in the right spot when they do."

Unlike their final on the Gold Coast, there are less

fireworks at Bells. Early in the heat, both Carissa and Steph fall, leading to below-average scores. With twenty minutes to go, Carissa holds a slim lead, but is vulnerable. Stephanie has the highest wave score of the heat and doesn't need much on her next wave to retake the lead. As the clock ticks down, it's a waiting game. I am certain that it is only a matter of time before a few rideable waves hit the Bells bowl.

Carissa is leading another Rip Curl Bells Beach final—her third consecutive. To many surfers, winning here, at one of the most storied venues in the sport, would be a defining moment in their career, but here Carissa is on the verge of winning the event for the third year in a row against a six-time defending world champion. Trying not to think about how painfully slow the clock is ticking, I think back to the time when things got serious for Carissa. I realized very early on in her competitive surfing experience that she had the talent to go far—as far as she could imagine. When she was nine years old I asked her what she wanted out of surfing.

"How good do you want to be?" I asked her.

"Dad, I want to be the best surfer in the world," she replied.

This was the response I was looking for, because I knew her verbal commitment would create a dialogue where I could explain what it would take to be the best.

I knew she had the talent. She was doing turns with more style and better technique than girls several years older. I knew I had the ability to explain things in a way she could understand. Though I was never a great surfer, I felt I knew enough about the sport to recognize what was important.

"Are you sure? If you want to be the best, you're not only going to have to work hard, but you're going to miss some things that your friends are doing. You'll get frustrated at times…and I am probably going to make you

41

cry," I responded. "You have the talent to be the best, and I can help you, so if you're sure, then let's go for it!"

"Dad, I'm sure. I want to be the best."

The journey began in earnest from that moment. Twelve years later, we find ourselves a world away at one of surfing's greatest venues, attempting to make history: ring the historic Bell three consecutive years. And on this day, for the remaining twenty minutes of the final, the ocean and fate are on her side—no waves with any scoring potential materialize. Carissa ends up winning one of the least exciting finals in her career. It's her second win of the year and she's rolling.

10

Instead of continuing on with Carissa to the third event, I head back to Oahu. It's a tough decision. She is, after all, on a roll. But I want to get back for Carissa's sister, Cayla. It's her last semester of high school and I want to be present as much as possible. That's probably the hardest part of all the travel. I can't be in two places at one time and don't feel like my seventeen-year-old daughter always gets a fair shake. This is my last window to watch her water polo games and to take her to surf-team competitions. It's her senior year and time's going way too fast. Before I know it she'll be out of the house and on her own.

Carissa knew this was coming. We discussed me missing a few events before the season started and the Drug Aware Margaret River Pro in Western Australia was one of the events I would be crossing off my list. In my absence I'm putting together a crack support crew to be there for her. The plan is to have her boyfriend, Luke, meet up with Carissa in Australia and use a local professional surfer, Andrew Sheridan, for coaching advice. Andrew's been by her side at the last two contests at Margaret River and helped propel her to back-to-back wins. I am confident that between Andrew's insight into the wave and its various moods and Luke there for moral support, Carissa has what she needs to succeed.

It's also a place Carissa feels very comfortable. Margaret River has a similar feel to the North Shore of Oahu in the way that the waves break. Storms off the southern tip of Africa churn and create huge swells that traverse the expansive Indian Ocean before crashing into the coast. Because the swell arrives from such a great distance, it has time to get more organized and travel with a longer-period interval. A long-period swell is generally going to have more energy, and thus the waves break with more power. That's why surfers from around the world flock to places like Western Australia and Hawaii. There's a lot of physics involved with wave creation, but in the simplest terms, the longer the interval, the bigger and more powerful the waves.

The waves around Margaret River are also a lot like what she rides back home in Hawaii in the sense that they break over shallow reefs. The bottom contours of the ocean—or bathymetry, as it's known—play a huge role in shaping how waves break. For example, beachbreaks typically break over sandbars, and because the sands shift up and down the beach with the currents, where and how the waves break is always changing. On the other hand, a reefbreak will break in pretty much the same place every time depending on what the tide and swell direction are doing. That's what makes somewhere like Margaret River or Pipeline in Hawaii unique and highly sought after by surfers. The consistency of a break is a huge factor that affects every surfer from the World Tour on down to the recreational folks.

On my way back home from Bells, I notice two giant storms forming off of the coast. Based on the forecast models, they're slated to push swell toward Western Australia for the first four days of the contest. It's all but guaranteed that the girls will be surfing in the big stuff. Large surf is an area in which Carissa has excelled in the past, but she's still nervous. Due to the commitments of travel and competition in the past two contests, she hasn't been able to practice in bigger waves. I am confident that she'll be able to handle the surf, but I know she'll need a few days to work herself into these serious and formidable conditions.

To add to it, she's worried that her boards might not be big enough for the largest days. I begin fretting over what she has available. Unlike the first contest, she won't have her shaper to solve any last-minute equipment issues.

It's part of the game that's especially challenging: trying to predict which boards to bring to cover the wide range of conditions she'll be facing. Before she left home we had to pack boards for two events in Australia with different conditions and wave sizes in mind. We discussed options and I did my best to give her an idea of what waves she should expect.

A quiver is a collection of different-sized boards that allow the surfer to step up or down in board size depending on the conditions. Like most surfers, Carissa will opt to ride a bigger board as the surf increases. Riding bigger boards has its advantages and disadvantages. Carissa understands that with each additional inch she will gain paddling speed and power. But it comes at the expense of maneuverability. In surf that's her height or under, she'll choose her smallest board length of 5'9"; as the surf increases, she'll add an inch for every additional foot or two in wave size. She has a wide range of boards to choose from, all the way up to ten feet in length. Her ten-foot "rhino chaser" barely turns, but it paddles well and allows her to catch some really big waves.

To add to the complexity of the board-packing equation, we had to factor in the real possibility of breaking a few boards along the way, especially in the bigger surf at Margaret River. The power of the surf can break a board in a fraction of a second, and having an adequate replacement is key. Before Carissa left for Bells, she stuffed two board bags with twelve surfboards of various shapes and sizes with the hopes she'd be covered.

In the days leading up to the event we talk about how her bigger boards are working. She tells me they're not handling the surf in the way that she likes. Arranging last-minute backup boards is a task that I usually handle, but I'm five thousand miles away. I suggest she talk with Andrew to help her find a few boards before the first round gets underway.

11

The girls are called to action on the third day of the waiting period. While the large swell has subsided a bit, the waves are still big. It's probably eight feet on the sets. From what I can tell from watching the webcast, some of the girls look scared. And for good reason: the surf is dangerous. Carissa grabs the biggest board she has and paddles out. She and her board perform well enough to win her first-round heat.

In a free-surf session after the round, Steph Gilmore suffers a serious wipeout. A wave hits her awkwardly and blows out her knee. She's forced to pull out of the contest and, now, for the foreseeable future, she's out of the world title race. Injuries are a very real part of the sport. It's something that every surfer has to contend with throughout the year.

Back at home I find myself in a strange coaching situation, as I am watching the event in real time via the computer and talking to Carissa about her upcoming heat. I do my best to give her confidence and leave the coaching duties to Andrew. After so many years of working so closely with Carissa and attending almost all of her events, not being at Carissa's side feels strange. There's a big part of me that wants to be there, but in my heart I know she needs to gain confidence and grow as a person. She can't do that if I'm always around her.

I have been making an effort to give her the room to grow as an athlete for some time now. In her early years, using her verbal commitment to be "the best surfer in the world" as the driving force, I used every opportunity to work with Carissa in and out of the surf. Between the ages of five and ten I surfed with Carissa every single time she set foot in the water. The effort was substantial, and in typical Chris Moore fashion, I've crunched the numbers as to how many waves I pushed her into during this time. Here's my math: thirty waves per day multiplied by five sessions a week multiplied by fifty-two weeks multiplied by five years equates to close to forty thousand waves. Those are some serious numbers.

When Carissa was nine years old, my wife, Carol, and I divorced. It wasn't an easy period for any of us and our decision-making became very polarized. One of the casualties of the divorce was that I could no longer take Carissa surfing whenever I liked. We now surfed together only when I had custody, three and a half days a week. Surfing time was further reduced because the one thing Carol and I did agree on was that Carissa would continue her education at Punahou, one of Oahu's top private schools.

These time constraints, in the long run, would be a mixed blessing. On one hand she couldn't surf every day, but on the other she learned time management and, most importantly, realized that in order to achieve her goals, she would have to make the best use of her time whenever she was in the water. Being that we had only small windows of time to practice, I felt I had to make use of as many of these opportunities as possible. Surfing became the priority.

Sleepovers and birthday parties posed a challenge. I always let Carissa attend, but felt she still should get her practice in. I would arrange to pick her up at dawn after a sleepover so we could squeeze in a morning session. Looking back, I question whether I needed to stress surfing as much as I did. I can see the benefits of it—she's now a world champion twice over—but I think I could have helped Carissa achieve the same goals with a less strict regimen. It's easy to second-guess my actions when it comes to my part in Carissa's surfing. I'm still somewhat conflicted by it all.

We've had difficult moments, but I've always tried my hardest to keep several factors in check. I tried to navigate these exchanges by asking myself why I was doing or saying something. What was the motivation? Was it selfish or selfless? I feel like the reason our relationship works is because in addition to wanting the best for Carissa, we both cherish our close connection. People often wonder why, especially in the earlier years, I would make a pile of sand in front of me while I was sitting on the beach watching her. Building sand pyramids was nothing more than a nervous tick that kept me from making any gestures or involving myself in any way in Carissa's performance during a heat.

I realized that any help I tried to give her during a heat was a distraction. I felt that whistling or motioning hand signals in an attempt to help her catch the right waves during a heat made me look silly. She needed to make decisions for herself. She needed to make mistakes and learn from them, too. Most of the time when I would second-guess a decision she was already way ahead of me. I would be thinking, "You should have paddled for that wave," and often she'd find a better wave shortly afterward. She was more often than not making better real-time decisions than I was making from the beach. The best thing I could do was to give her confidence and trust her. We learned. We improved. The results came.

12

After her initial surfboard crisis in Margaret River, Carissa hits her stride. After all our fretting she finds a board that she's confident on, and in classic West Oz conditions with big, open-faced waves and stiff offshore winds, she blitzes her way straight to the final and is now matched up against California's Courtney Conlogue.

By no means is a clash with Courtney a new thing. She and Carissa have been competing against one another since they were ten years old. The first time they met was at Lower Trestles a surf break located in Southern California during the annual National Scholastic Surfing Association (NSSA) championships. At the time they shared the same sponsor, Roxy, and I could tell even back then that a bit of a rivalry was developing between the two girls. They were both so competitive and driven. It had to be.

They'd both entered the co-ed 10 and Under Mini Grom division. At the time it was completely dominated by the best up-and-coming boys in the country. Just the same, both Carissa and Courtney battled their way into the semifinals. Carissa ended up advancing to the final while Courtney fell just short. I still remember how disappointed she appeared. For being so young, she was already extremely competitive. From what I could tell, Courtney wanted to win. It's a trait that has served her well as her career has blossomed.

For the next six years the two girls surfed against each other countless times, drawing the absolute best out of each other along the way. By the time they were eighteen, they were both ready to graduate to the World Championship Tour, and today it's safe to say that Courtney is one of Carissa's fiercest rivals.

In the final at Margaret River, Courtney's full speed ahead. She's attacking the waves with a hunger and passion that's all too familiar. Time and again you see how critical passion is. At this level, everybody has an exorbitant amount of talent, but it's getting in that rhythm with the emotions and the conditions that can be a real difference-maker.

For thirty-five minutes the two girls surf their hearts out. Holding anything back means a guaranteed loss, a fact Carissa and Courtney are all too aware of. In the end, Courtney finds better waves and surfs them with the same fervor as that ten-year-old we met so many years ago. Courtney is definitely in rhythm, and seeing how much she's putting into her surfing, I get the feeling we're going to be dealing with her a lot more this season. The victory is hers. With the runner-up finish, Carissa leaves Australia with two firsts and a second, as strong a lead in the world-title race as I could reasonably ask for.

13

When Carissa and Luke touch down after their twelve-hour flight from Australia, I'm at the airport to meet them. It's hugs all around, but our minds are already on the upcoming Oi Rio Pro in Rio de Janeiro, Brazil. Carissa has a week at home before she heads back to Honolulu International Airport for her flight to South America, and there's work to be done.

First order of business: she's going to need to adjust her approach to better fit the tricky surf conditions she'll be facing in Rio. It will be the first Tour event of the year where Carissa has to surf a beachbreak. The beachbreaks in Rio aren't much different than beachbreaks found anywhere else in the world, but after focusing her energies on surfing right-hand point- and reefbreaks in Australia, it's going to take some getting used to. The surf in Rio fluctuates considerably depending on swell height and direction, tides, and the ever-changing contour of the sand below. There are distinct differences in approaching a heat in these conditions. It can be a hard game to play.

Work starts with replicating scenarios on Oahu that will give Carissa confidence when she performs in the South Atlantic seascape. One of the biggest things I have to keep in mind is that the beachbreaks in Rio will give her opportunities to go either right or left on the waves— approaching the waves on both her forehand and backhand. For the past three events Carissa's been competing on relatively predictable right-hand-breaking waves, so the first order of business is to get her back to riding lefts. For that, we spend time at two of her favorite lefts, Ala Moana

Bowls and Kewalo Basin on the South Shore.

I accompany Carissa on most of her sessions during the week and spend time watching and taking mental notes. It's a stark contrast from our earlier years, when I spent most of our sessions out in the water with her, giving her constant feedback. Now feedback comes only when she paddles in, and my comments are much shorter and simpler. Lately I have been looking less at the technical aspects and more at the emotional side of her surfing. I focus on the feeling I get when she surfs. Is she pushing her turns and putting effort into her performance? Can I feel her effort? I see similarities between surfing and dancing in this regard. When I watch a good dance performance, I get excited. And with Carissa, I focus on how I feel when she's performing on a wave. I know when she surfs with her heart that it can be emotional and exciting; likewise, I can feel when her surfing is tentative or uninspired.

We talk about this a lot when she finishes her workouts. We still have some tricky conversations, but it is a far cry from a few years ago, when the dad/coach line often got crossed. It would start innocently enough, but every so often I would say something, a simple critique that Carissa didn't want to hear, and like that we were butting heads again. I was the type of coach that wouldn't settle for fussing. For years I would argue back when she got upset with something I said. After so many failed discussions, it became pretty easy for both of us to push each other's buttons. Today things don't go that far. Our discussions are far from perfect, but we rarely push each other the way we used to.

"Carissa, I think your surfing right now is *brilliant*," I say after a session a couple of days before the start of the Rio Pro. "Your backside turns are spot-on and your flow is seamless. The only thing is I would like to see you pull into barrels a little more often when you have the chance."

The last sentence riles her up. She snaps back, "So

53

you don't like my surfing?!"

For years this is where I would get frustrated and argue back. Though I'm a bit annoyed by her remarks, I look at her calmly and say, "Carissa, I used the word 'brilliant' to describe your surfing today. I certainly love what you are doing. Let's discuss this more later."

I maintain my calm demeanor until I get in the car and drive away. Luckily, we came to the beach in separate cars. I'm able to make an easy getaway without any further buttons being pushed. Moments later I get a phone call and an apology. All is well. She's as ready for Brazil as she's going to be.

14

For the second time in as many contests, I won't be attending the event. Carissa's beau, Luke, is also out. The plan is to line up another support team to travel with her. We're looking at an unproven, yet very trustworthy, group. Pro surfer turned Hurley vice president Pat O'Connell's going to be her coach. He was on Tour for years and will be making the trip down to South America to help her with lineups. Luke's mom, Lori, will be stepping in for emotional support. With the coaching duties on Pat and the love coming from Lori, I hope Carissa's set for South America.

One of the major challenges when Carissa's in Brazil is communicating with a seven-hour time difference. She will be practicing and competing when it's the middle of the night in Hawaii. I've never been very good between the hours of midnight and five in the morning. This time there will be way less talking immediately before and after heats, and when we do, it's bound to be a lot less coherent—and enthusiastic—on my end.

I do my best to talk with her in the days leading up to the contest about staying focused and positive. Carissa tells me that the beachbreak in Barra da Tijuca, the beach town in which the contest will be held, is tricky and that most of the waves are closeouts. She knows that she will have to be very attentive to conditions in order to track down the best waves, as the ocean and weather conditions seem to be in constant flux.

Carissa will also have to deal with competing in front of a loud and raucous Brazilian crowd. Last year,

Gabriel Medina became the first Brazilian to win a WSL men's world title, which has elevated him to the level of mega sports star there. Carissa will have to contend with a crowd that's more excited than any other on Tour. Thankfully it's old hat when it comes to dealing with tricky and uncomfortable situations. She's been competing and performing under pressure for years.

In Carissa's teenage years, there was no shortage of opportunities to surf in high-profile competitions. Besides the monthly NSSA contests, there was a lengthy calendar of world-tour qualifying events, world junior amateur championships, and national championships. I could have entered Carissa in all of these events, but she would have been surfing in contests virtually nonstop.

Because there were so many opportunities to surf, I felt I could cherry pick events that suited her and pass on others that didn't fit into our program. Opting for contests that suited Carissa, I was cognizant of putting her in situations where she would have a chance to evolve and grow but also succeed. I often chose fun and easy right-hand pointbreak waves like Snapper Rocks, or I would stick close to home and place her in events that were held at a break where she felt comfortable.

My initial hope was that by putting Carissa in some of these kinds of high-pressure environments, I could create a situation where she was too young to realize the implications of her circumstances and thus feel more normal about it all as she grew up. For similar reasons, I entered her in boys' competitions. When she competed in "boys only" events, she wasn't necessarily wanted—she was alone and scrutinized—but, being so young, she never second-guessed my decision. She just went along with it and surfed.

I saw additional benefits to surfing against the boys. I thought it would be an interesting challenge for her in the respect that she would have to step up her game to advance.

The boys were not only better competition, but they were also more aggressive—and none of them wanted to lose to a girl. So I pushed Carissa to keep pace with the boys and success came.

When she was fifteen she competed in the Quiksilver King of the Groms, a surf event featuring Hawaii's top boys under the age of sixteen. Carissa's sponsor at the time was Roxy, the sister brand to Quiksilver, so it was easy for me to "sneak" her into the event. Quiksilver was happy to accommodate. After all, if she did well it was good publicity for the brand.

My instinct told me this was a smart event for her to compete in. The site of the annual contest was Kewalo Basin, where, during the summer months, she surfed almost daily alongside many of the boys in the event. This was a spot where Carissa was comfortable and confident—the two C's that have long been part of her recipe for success.

By now Carissa had no problem surfing with and against her male peers. Carissa was a good surfer and the boys knew it, so there was a level of respect she'd earned. In addition, by this point she had been surfing against the boys for so long—though I am sure they were sometimes less than pleased with her attendance—that they were used to her entering competitions and getting the better of them.

We looked at it as a no-lose situation. I told her that, being a girl, no one expected her to do well, and besides, "it's good practice" and "you get to be the underdog." She wholeheartedly took on the challenge. She knew that when she surfed against the girls there was an expectation and pressure to win, but against the boys there was never any expectation, and certainly no pressure to win.

For the King of the Groms, I prepared her to win. Carissa was excited to surf—a bad omen for the Hawaiian boys. The waves at Kewalos showed up, too. They were big and well shaped. It was one of the best days of the summer. There was a lot of scoring potential for both the turn sections and the barrels. Carissa found both. In the semifinals she rode one of the best barrels she's ever caught out at the break, a full, deep backdoor drainer that completely engulfed her for a moment. It was enough to win the heat and send her into the final.

In the finals, she was patient. This particular contest featured a one-wave "claim" format in which a surfer raised their hands after a completed ride to signify to the judges that they wanted that score counted for their heat. But once they claimed, their heat was over. One by one, the boys claimed average scores, and with their claim, they had to paddle in. Carissa was left sitting out the back alone for the last five minutes of the heat. She knew exactly what type of wave she was looking for. The waiting paid off. A set loomed; she took off and ripped the wave all the way through until it petered out into the channel. She claimed it. Victory was hers.

Unlike the previous year, there was no formal presentation. There was no lining up and announcing of final results. There was a rushed trophy handoff and that was it. Peering dejectedly from a distance, the boys were in such disarray that not a single one of them was in a mood to celebrate. Kewalo Basin was a very somber place that day. There would be no King of the Groms, but there would be a queen.

15

As the contest in Rio begins, Carissa starts to feel the pressures of being in a fan-frenzied environment. Brazil offers a different type of fan. Many are looking for something. Usually it's a simple photo, but there are also requests for hats, jerseys, shirts, leashes, you name it. For Carissa, these requests make her uncomfortable.

We both know it comes with the territory of being in the position she's in. She knows sometimes it's best just to keep the head down and make it to the beach and surf. Of course, the surf is doing its best to throw her as well. After a frustrating first round, I get a concerned call from Carissa. She tells me she's having trouble figuring out the break. There are lots of sand-sucking closeout sections, making it hard for her to do a proper turn. It's hard for me to give her any real coaching pointers from where I'm sitting back in the valley on Oahu, but I talk to her about being confident in her abilities. I have told her many times that her speed and technique make her a very good beachbreak surfer. Her simple ability to stand up quickly, a basic talent that is so often overlooked, gives her a distinct advantage. She's one of the best in the world at this simple move. Carissa also has tremendously fast reflexes. She's very good at popping up and placing her feet right where they need to be on the board. This enables her to set up and get into her first turn quickly. In a beachbreak scenario, you want to have as much setup time as possible, because so many waves run down the line or quickly close out.

On the beach, Pat O'Connell is there to help her. He's a talented beachbreak specialist who actually delayed going on Tour a year so he could star in *The Endless Summer II*, the same film that inspired Carissa's whole journey. For the most part Carissa is fine on her own at this event, but with the shifty waves and constantly changing weather conditions it's good to have a second pair of eyes. Having Pat there gives Carissa good peace of mind going into her heats.

The complexity of surfing a thirty-minute heat is hard enough when the waves are good, but when the conditions are tricky and the crowd on the beach is going nuts, finding two good waves in that amount of time can be daunting. Carissa does her best to find scores and advances through the early rounds. Despite her success, I am wary because I know the difficulties involved with putting solid heat totals together round after round, especially in these conditions. So much of her talent advantage is erased because of the luck factor involved. Rip currents can destroy a peak in minutes and create others a football field away. If you're not at the right place at the right time, all the surfing talent in the world won't make a difference.

At home I'm developing jet lag without flying. Waking up multiple times each night for heat checks throws my sleep pattern off significantly. I am glad I don't have to say much more to her than "good job" or "make sure you check with Pat before your heat." Carissa makes it to the semifinals before losing to South African Bianca Buitendag. For the effort, she walks away with a third-place finish.

Meanwhile, Courtney Conlogue wins her second event of the year to close the gap on the world-title race. Looking at the next few events on Tour, the advantage could swing in Courtney's favor. Coming up next is the heavy surf of Fiji and then two back-to-back events in Courtney's home state of California. All of a sudden it's looking like the title race is going to be a hard-fought battle.

16

Through her season started strong, I think both of us wanted more. I would have liked to see more of a cushion for my daughter going into the next event of the Tour, the Fiji Pro. Carissa will not be the favorite here, especially if the surf gets really big.

We will be staying on the tiny island of Tavarua, not far from the main island of Fiji. Dubbed "a heart-shaped island in the Pacific," it is one of the most idyllic and beautiful locations in the world. Since its discovery by surfers in the late '70s, it's become one of those locations that wave riders dream about, and a stay at the resort on the island costs about three thousand dollars a week. Unfortunately, we are not there for rest and relaxation. Our week on Tavarua will most certainly be no vacation. This event will be challenging and will test Carissa's resolve. The wave at Cloudbreak offers a large, barreling left-hander with an expansive takeoff zone. The best waves wall up and look unmakeable. Success here is more psychological than physical.

The wave is located on a reef two miles out to sea from the main island, so triangulating landmarks to establish position in the lineup is thrown out the window. There is a permanent judging scaffolding built onto the reef that Carissa can use, but it's still tricky. It's a break that takes a lot of practice in addition to a large dose of courage to become comfortable.

To help prepare for this event, Carissa flew over in January with world champion bodyboarder Mike Stewart to work on her barrel riding at the break. For waves like

Cloudbreak, positioning—taking off on the right part of the wave in order to surf it properly—is everything. I had hoped that Mike would pass on some of his knowledge and experience to Carissa. The trip was a success; in addition to learning more about Cloudbreak, she had the opportunity to spend time with and learn from a great wave rider.

For the actual event we're bringing in Hawaiian power surfer and former World Tour competitor Pancho Sullivan to help her with positioning and strategy. Pancho had been instrumental in helping Carissa win her first WSL event in 2009 at Sunset Beach on the North Shore of Oahu. This win was a big step in Carissa's evolution in professional surfing and was the first time she used a specialty coach to help at a contest.

I knew that I would never be much help when it came to assisting Carissa at Sunset Beach. I grew up on the South Shore of the island, and when I did drive over to the North Shore, I'd usually surf somewhere closer to Haleiwa, rarely making it past Ehukai Beach Park in my quest for waves. Sunset Beach had a reputation for being a scary and challenging surf spot. Large winter swells throw mountains of water into the ever-shifting two-hundred-yard expanse of reef. I've never understood the dynamics of this break due to my lack of water time there, which translated into a string of poor results for my daughter.

I knew I needed help to get Carissa to step up her performance at Sunset. Fortunately, in 2009, two professional surfers—Pancho Sullivan and Myles Padaca—created a program called "Progressive Surfing," which provided coaching to aspiring surfers on Oahu. Both surfers had tremendous success on the North Shore and Sunset Beach in particular. I thought it would be a great fit and that Carissa would really benefit from the knowledge that they'd be able to impart.

The effort to win would be substantial. We put in place a lengthy and detailed schedule where Carissa would meet up with her coaches on the North Shore in the months leading up to the event. They would practice out at Sunset and go over which waves to look for depending on the swell size and direction. Pancho and Myles pointed out markers on land she could reference for an idea of where to sit. They taught her which wave to look for while navigating rogue waves and strong currents in the lineup, located about a quarter mile out to sea. Their years of studying and hands-on experience in the lineup helped accelerate her learning and gave her the needed confidence to compete at the break.

In the span of one year, Carissa, at the age of seventeen, went from losing the trials to winning her first WCT event against the best female surfers in the world in large and difficult surf at Sunset Beach. We brought Pancho onboard for Fiji because we needed to have a similar approach at Cloudbreak.

In the days leading up to the event, I notice her anticipation and nervousness intensifying, as she knows that not only does she have the world-title chase to contend with, but she also has a wave of consequence looming before her. No number of pep talks and motivational speeches will make a difference for what's in store for her on the reef at Cloudbreak. The bigger it gets, the scarier and more powerful the wave becomes. Though she has the talent and ability to handle these extreme conditions, overcoming the fear factor is key to faring well.

As much as I want her to challenge herself, I can't make her perform. It's conflicting being a parent in situations like this. The coach in me wants to push her to do everything to win. The dad in me wants to make sure she's safe and comfortable. That's all compounded at somewhere like Tavarua, where the waves can really be dangerous.

The dangers are real. The waves get big. And they're powerful. South swells rumble up to Fiji from storms generated in the world's nether regions, and it's with this unbridled force that the energy collides into the open-ocean reef at Cloudbreak. Universally it's considered a dream wave, but that doesn't make it any less gnarly.

Last year, Tour rookie Nikki Van Dijk hit the reef during her heat and she had to withdraw from the contest. She ended up with bruised ribs and a busted lip which required sixteen stitches and plastic surgery. She's not the only girl to have gotten mangled there. It's the game they play; if Carissa wants to be successful here, there's no getting around it.

17

The best remedy for her situation is to move up our travel plans and head to Fiji a few days early. Our goal will be to work out the jitters and get reacquainted with the break.

Our change of plans means that Carissa and I are on our own for a few days before Pancho is scheduled to arrive. As luck would have it, we paddle into larger and more challenging surf than we had expected on our first session. For some reason, surfing right after traveling is always difficult. It's nice to be able to ease into things, but that's not always how this sport works. Part of me wants to just sit back and let Carissa work herself into the new conditions, but then there's the coach in me that wants to challenge her to push herself. I know the swell is forecasted to drop over the next few days and feel that if she is going to get some practice in serious conditions, now is her chance.

The lineup is almost empty, but sometimes the lack of a crowd can pose a problem for Carissa. Other surfers in the water help her figure out where to sit, and when she sees one of her friends on a good one, it always gets her fired up. With nobody out, she has a tendency to be too selective. I know that if she gets too picky, she'll end up sitting too much, so I challenge her to take a few chances. My logic is that it will be best to get some rides (and some wipeouts) and for her to realize that she can handle the conditions she is facing, in turn giving her more confidence. I paddle out with her and help position her in the critical takeoff zone, but when the bigger set waves pulse through, she paddles away from where she needs to be. She's spooked by what she's feeling in the water. I do my best to settle her down. She's not happy with my plan of playing this game of aquatic chicken. She's smart enough to know that if she wants to do well here, she will have to push herself more than she normally would like.

"Look, Carissa, you have to go for some of the ones that look like they are going to close out. They're the ones that are running down the line," I say.

She gives me the "you're crazy" look and I realize I am probably pushing her too much on the first day out. My feelings of wanting to really challenge her to the point of getting her upset start to surface. Carissa recognizes the situation too.

"Dad, stop pushing me. Let me figure this out for myself for a while," she tells me.

I follow her command and relegate myself to the channel, where I watch the rest of her practice. I know she wants the push that I can give her, but there's always that fine line we walk. Sometimes she just needs to hear it from another source.

18

Pancho arrives the day before the contest and handles the next session. He keeps it light and simple.

"Let's focus on looking for takeoff spots and try to feel comfortable out in the water," he tells Carissa.

Carissa responds, doing a better job of trusting her ability and paddling into some waves that she wasn't trying the day before. I leave the two alone and once again hang out in the channel. Progress.

I am happy with her improvement out in the lineup. She looks great, especially when she pulls into a few big barrels. I'm impressed, but not surprised. I know she has the ability. We've worked on this part of her surfing for years. She has developed very sound technique when it comes to riding a barrel, though it's a part of her surfing that she has struggled with because she's been somewhat wary of trying.

Years ago, rather than pulling under the curl, she would almost always opt to either ride past the barreling section, straighten out, or do a turn. This would frustrate me, and during some sessions I would end up giving her strict instructions only to set up and ride the barrel. She'd respond, practice, and improve, often immediately. Despite her improvement and the thrill of accomplishment, without continued instruction in a few days she'd eventually fade back to barrel dodging. I'd again challenge her, and again progress would come. These are the kinds of issues that challenge both of us.

Unlike the waiting we endured in Australia, at the Fiji Pro the contest gets underway on the second day of the holding period. The waves are big, but not too scary. Carissa surfs with confidence and commitment and puts together some big scores to advance. I feel good about her progress in the few days she's been here. It's certainly an improvement since last year.

On the island of Tavarua, the Red Bull–sponsored Jet Ski I'd arranged for Carissa and Pancho to use during the contest has shown up and is anchored just offshore. A month ago I had an idea that having our own ski would give Carissa an edge. She could shuttle in and out from the break as she pleased rather than waiting for the boats from Tavarua, which stay out there for hours at a time. Though it arrived at the island a few days late, I was happy that she'd be able to use it for the remainder of the contest.

At least I thought it was going to be a nice addition. The first thing I noticed when I checked it was that the battery had died. It was getting dark and I figured I'd handle it in the morning. By morning the engine was completely flooded and the ski was in danger of sinking. Now, instead of darting out to the surf, I had to babysit a waterlogged Jet Ski. While Pancho and Carissa went out to practice—on the shuttle boats, like everyone else—I was busy trying to figure out how to drag this piece of junk up the beach and what the hell to do with it. I had to laugh. It was one of my brilliant ideas that had somehow completely blown up in my face.

In the next round, which is a non-elimination heat, Carissa makes a few tactical errors. Most significantly, she kicks out early on one of her highest-scoring waves, which ends up being the difference between first and second. Back at her room, dejected, she lies in bed for most of the afternoon. When I talk to her I realize she's lost the confidence she's amassed over the past four contests. That's all it took. One misstep and we're all of a sudden teetering on the brink.

It's like déjà vu. She was in the same exact position

going into Fiji last year. She was on top of the leaderboard and Cloudbreak really shook up her confidence. Last year was hard for me to watch, and though there have been many times in her professional surfing career when I have witnessed breakdowns in confidence, last year was her biggest one. It was agonizing to see her go through that mid-season slump, and, to a degree, I stayed away from really pushing her to snap out of it. I figured she needed to sort things out herself.

Yet here we are, looking right back into another possible slump, and right now I don't have the right words for her. At this point even the best words probably wouldn't do much to turn things around. Cloudbreak has rattled both of us over the past few years, and though she has made special trips to surf the break and has been surfing well during recent free-surfs, I have an uneasy feeling.

The morning of the final day is dark and moody. The weather is overcast and the ocean looks angry. Carissa has a good warm-up but finds herself in a bind when Pancho breaks her 6'6" backup board while duck-diving under a wave. This has left both Carissa and I in a bit of a panic. Two of her big-wave boards are now broken and two others are not responding the way that she'd hoped. She's down to two boards.

Though I can tell that she's bothered by the morning's events, I do my best to give her some space. She does her best to turn her head around, but it seems that the ocean is against her. In the early minutes of her next heat, a routine wipeout snaps Carissa's leash and she loses her board. While spending time retrieving it, she falls behind as her competitor, Californian Lakey Peterson, picks off a good wave. Eventually getting back out into the lineup, Carissa battles back to regain the lead with just a couple minutes left on the clock. This is big for her in so many ways. I'm relieved and proud; she fought back and with time about to expire she looks assured of a quarterfinal berth.

Or not. With seconds left on the clock, Lakey finds a wave. She tears into it. It's enough to win the heat and devastate my daughter. We immediately head back to the island. Carissa throws herself down on her bed and sobs. We both know that she tried her best and didn't back down. I know I can overanalyze, and I have been scolded by Carissa in the past for not being comforting enough during times like this, so back on the beach I give her a long hug. We don't argue or replay what happened. I feel for her and let her cycle through her emotions. She tried her best. At times like this, the coach in me disappears and it's just dad. All I can do is feel for her.

Sally Fitzgibbons goes on to win the event. Sally suffered a perforated eardrum in an earlier round and continued to surf despite the event doctor's objections. Though she was in obvious pain, she simply duct taped a swim cap to her head, strapped on a helmet and paddled back out to her next heat.

With her victory, she has placed herself into world-title contention with Carissa and Courtney at the halfway mark of the season. Courtney was eliminated in the quarterfinals, which is fortunate for us because she wasn't able to get out in front of the ratings. There's a lot of love and camaraderie between the girls on Tour, but Sally and Courtney, if they get a whiff of weakness they'll go for the throat. That's competition. Our job now is to head back home, regroup, and not let a little setback derail us. We have to remember that Carissa's still fronting the ratings with two wins to her credit and it's a long season.

19

It is a good time to be back home. Cayla's senior year is coming to a close and both Carissa and I spend time with her in the days leading up to her graduation. Like me, Carissa's aware she's missed much of her sister's high school years. Even with everything swirling around the world-title race, we focus our attention and energy on what Cayla needs. It's a good distraction.

Other than getting ready for graduation, Cayla is going through her final preparations for the upcoming NSSA High School National Surfing Championships in Dana Point, California. For the past four years she's been on the high school surf team, and this will be her final contest. Surfing with the team has been a great outlet that's allowed Cayla to continue to develop her surfing while Carissa and I are on the road. She's carved out a unique path for herself, and this year she's team captain.

The experience with the team has been a godsend. With the disproportionate amount of time I've spent with Carissa over the years, combined with the world titles and abundance of success, it's long been a fear of mine that it would all have a negative effect on Cayla. I know guilt had something to do with it. For years I've felt really guilty about the time away from home and not being there for my younger daughter. It scared me that she might become jealous, or give up, or act up out of frustration. There are so many directions a teenager can turn. My fears went as far as pondering if she'd turn to drugs, or sex, or something else simply because I wasn't there. I tried my best to compensate when I returned home after long trips, but there's always been a nagging feeling that somehow I fell short in giving her enough time.

But perhaps I got lucky. Perhaps I did just enough to keep Cayla happy and confident. And I know I had help. Carissa and her are tight. This bond between sisters has had a lot to do with keeping her balanced.

Cayla is almost five years younger than Carissa, and when she was little and Carissa and I were on the road, she usually stayed home with her mom. Her mom wasn't too stoked on our surfing routine, so when we were out of town Cayla would often end up dry-docked until we came home. Because of this, she figured out how to blaze her own trail. Subsequently, she developed a more independent approach to surf training. When she and I did practice together, if she got confused or frustrated with something I was trying to teach her, she wouldn't think twice about telling me she wanted to figure things out on her own. More than a few times she'd end a training session by telling me to paddle in.

"Go away, Dad! You're frustrating me!" she'd tell me in the lineup.

My gut reaction was to force her to listen by scolding her. But there was no getting around it. If she didn't want my advice, she wasn't going to listen. I couldn't employ the same tactics I used with Carissa. I simply had to put my ego aside and let her either figure it out herself or wait for her to come back to me when she was ready to listen to my suggestions. Cayla's independence flourished when she joined the high school surf team. Team members and coaches became her support network. Throughout high school she had the opportunity to surf, even when Carissa and I weren't there for her. Knowing this made traveling and being away from her a little easier.

In the days leading up to nationals, I get in a routine of surfing with Cayla and the team whenever I can. She's looking strong and confident. But again, Cayla wants to do things her way and on her terms. When the time comes to travel, she opts for me to stay home. Sometimes I wonder how two kids from the same parents can be wired so differently.

"Dad, I'd like you to stay home. I'm fine going by myself and doing this with the team," she tells me.

I know she'll be fine without me. After all, I was told to stay home last year, too, and it worked out fine. She ended up winning the girls' national title. Relegated to the sidelines, I do my best to check in each day. I can tell she is excited, and whenever possible, I still throw tidbits of advice at her. She probably can go on and do her thing with no problem at all without me bugging her on the phone every day, but she listens and thanks me each time.

On the afternoon of the last day of the competition, I get a call.

"Dad! I won! We won!"

Cayla has won her second straight individual and team national title. For me, personally, there's solace in knowing my two girls have accomplished so much—that somehow maybe this whole crazy parenting high-wire act I'm trying to pull off is actually working.

20

After almost two months off, Carissa and I land in Los Angeles for the sixth event on the WSL calendar, the U.S. Open of Surfing in Huntington Beach. When we arrive, summer vacation is in full swing in Surf City USA. Thousands of people are here to watch, hang out, and party. There is no shortage of distractions for fans and non-fans alike. Besides the surf contest, there are towering vert ramps for skateboard and BMX contests, a large outdoor concert stage, and several thousand square feet of air-conditioned retail shops. The surf and action-sports industries are centered in Orange County, and over the years this contest has been billed as the "greatest show in surf."

Financially it makes sense; more people equates to bigger sponsorship dollars. The way I see it, the desire for the best surf possible is secondary, but it's understandable. Sponsorship dollars and large viewership are necessary to keep the professional surfing machine running. Some events on Tour, like Fiji, sell the surfer's dream of a perfect, empty wave breaking off a tropical island in the middle of the Pacific. The U.S. Open is not this. This is pop culture. This is max marketing dollars. This is "the industry" pulling out all the stops.

I don't like the crowds and the vibe that comes with it. Frankly, I don't like the surf here either. Huntington is a place I kept Carissa away from when she was young. The break doesn't really suit her style. Both the lineup and the beach are crowded. We both get claustrophobic. Around contest time it's a place that wears on us mentally.

As she matured, I knew she needed the experience here, so we started to make some inroads into understanding the tricky break a little better. Because so many people attend the event and so much is going on around it, Carissa's sponsors wanted the attention she would bring. When we started coming to Huntington, the U.S. Open was a highly ranked qualifying contest, so no matter what, the road to a successful surfing career would take her through Surf City.

Like always, figuring out the best positioning in the water is going to be a challenge, much like it was at the Oi Rio Pro earlier in the year. Like the beaches in Barra de Tijuca, Huntington is shifty. It breaks over a shallow sandbar near a large pier that juts several hundred yards into the Pacific. Depending on the swell direction, the tide, and the contour of the sandbar, waves on the south side of the pier—the location of the contest area—are either peaky or walled. It also has a nasty tendency to get windy and blown out by midday, which only complicates matters. And if a strong south swell is running, the current will start pulling down the beach, making it practically impossible to hold your position in the lineup.

Another thing that makes the U.S. Open unique is that unlike any of the other contests on Tour, there is no waiting period. Because the Open is as much circus as surf contest, it has to adhere to a predetermined, set schedule—a stark contrast to the contests where the surfers' representatives choose the best times to surf. In Huntington, heats will run like clockwork from morning until late afternoon for a week straight. Carissa's heat will run when scheduled regardless of weather or ocean conditions.

In order to prepare, before we left Hawaii we spent most of our water time practicing at Sandy Beach. Sandy's offers conditions similar to Huntington. Located on the southeast corner of Oahu, the break is exposed to the prevailing trade winds more than most spots where Carissa normally practices. Blustery conditions combined with an uneven bottom contour makes for constantly changing wave faces. Like Huntington, Sandy's is also tricky and frustrating. During many practices, Carissa surfed wave after wave without success, but with perseverance she was able to put together a few dynamic moves. I was pleased with her success rate and told her she just had to remain positive. The magic would happen if she kept trying.

21

In the days leading up to the Open, Carissa maintains her edge. It's not easy. Practicing in the contest area next to the pier, the waves are small and it's hard to find rhythm in the schizophrenic conditions. I choose my words properly in her post-practice assessments in hopes of building confidence. The challenge is to give her information without her second guessing my feedback or to let any of my frustration show when things aren't going the way I'd like.

Something as simple as saying "You looked as good as you could out there" is a potential recipe for disaster. Hypersensitivity has snuck into our world-title equation. I find myself scrutinizing and overthinking much of what I have to say. Before anything comes out of my mouth, I wrestle with how she might misinterpret what I am saying. It's far from ideal, but for the time being, I feel it's what needs to be done to keep a semblance of sanity.

I gently remind her that she can do only what the waves allow. I talk with her about focusing on the challenge and finding enjoyment in performing the best she can regardless of what the ocean is throwing at her. Surfing is a game. Breaking it down to the most basic level, all anyone is trying to do is go out and outscore their competitor. At the end of the heat, the person with the most points wins. It's as simple as that. It's easy to get misled into thinking that every heat has to be a home-run performance. It doesn't. It just has to be better than whomever is in the water with you at the moment.

Whether it's something I've said or just something

she's figured out herself, going into the contest, Carissa's mood is light and easygoing. Maybe it's because she knows she has been successful here. She's won the event twice, but I'm still far from certain how things will play out. Huntington's a place where I've come to expect the unexpected.

Two years ago, Carissa looked about as rattled as I have ever seen her before a surf contest. Her timing was off. She barely completed a turn in warm-up. She had breakdowns in her hotel room and on the beach before and after practices, yet when it came time to compete, she found a way to battle through heats. She ended up winning the event that year, and it proved to be instrumental in helping her secure her second world title. Last year was the opposite. She looked great going into the event and ended up posting her worst result of the year, a ninth-place finish, which sent her deeper into her mid-season slump.

In the opening round of this year's contest, Carissa faces Australian Nikki Van Dijk. Before the heat, we have a tough decision to make. There are several different peaks, and nailing down our strategy is tricky. We roll the dice and decide on the peak that's breaking closest to the pier. Carissa's strategy seems to pay off as she finds a few mid-range scores. I like what she's doing, but her short rides don't allow a breakaway and the heat remains tight. Despite Carissa surfing her waves to the best of her ability, Nikki finds a better wave on a different peak down the beach to squeak out a win. Carissa is rattled. I'm frustrated. Even though there were no real flaws in the strategy or surfing, this déjà vu thing is starting to get annoying.

Carissa now has the "losers' round" to contend with. She's not out of this thing yet, but she needs to get her head straight.

22

At times, I wish I could go back in time and draw from past magic. While Carissa struggles in Huntington, I think back to one of our early trips to Mexico. It was a simpler time when there was no overthinking or stressing. She had just turned fifteen and everything seemed to be falling into place.

We had traveled to San Miguel for a specialty contest the NSSA had newly created that was running in conjunction with a low-rated Men's World Qualifying Series professional event where Carissa was the only female in a field of men. Located in Northern Baja, San Miguel is a right-hand cobblestone pointbreak—just the type of break I knew she could do something with if given a proper chance.

A month prior, upon hearing that the NSSA was sponsoring this event, I immediately had an idea: get Carissa in both the NSSA specialty and men's professional events. Simple in theory, but in all practicality there was no guarantee she'd get into either one, as both events were reserved specifically for men. It hadn't fazed me in my attempts to have her surf with the boys up until this point; why should it now? Plus, I had a plan and I was fairly certain I could pull it off.

The plan was to get Carissa into the NSSA-sponsored event first and then finagle her into the professional event when we got down to the contest site in Mexico. I figured I had a reasonable chance to get Carissa in, as she was the all-time NSSA record holder and had just won her tenth and eleventh titles just a few weeks prior. All

I needed to do was ask. I called the head of the NSSA, Janice Aragon.

"Janice, hi, this is Chris Moore, Carissa's dad. Carissa saw that you are holding an event down in Mexico next month and she wanted me to ask you if she could surf in it."

"Well, I'm sorry, but there's no girls' event this time around. Maybe next year," Janice replied.

I knew going into the conversation that this was a boys-only deal, so I was prepared for my counter: "Carissa said she'd love to surf with the boys!" I figured Janice wouldn't need any further convincing, as she had been a big supporter of Carissa's surfing throughout her amateur career.

Janice thought about it for a second and said, "I really didn't think about having a girl in the contest, but she certainly deserves it. OK, we'll put her in."

Now that she was in, I had to convince my daughter, which I knew would be no problem.

"Hey, Carissa! Janice Aragon of the NSSA called me and invited you to a new event in Mexico. It's going to feature the best surfers in the NSSA and she chose you as the only girl! And guess what? It's going to be at a right-hand pointbreak; it'll be sooo fun! And good practice!"

Carissa was sold; besides, she trusted me.

"Really, I'll be the only girl? OK, I'm in!"

My con game was in full swing. Feeling bold, I made a call to Carissa's Roxy team manager.

"Hey, guess what? Carissa is invited to an event in Mexico where she'll be the only girl against a field of men. It'll be great PR for the brand, don't you think? Do you have anything left in the budget for some airline tickets and hotel reservations?"

Roxy was never an easy sell.

"Well, I'm not sure. You've already maxed out your travel budget for the year."

I'd dealt with this before. I was sure a little more coaxing was all that was needed.

"Think about it. She'll be the only girl. That's instant PR right there."

"Alright, we'll handle it," was their response.

"Oh yeah, and can we get a little per diem for a car and food?"

"Ugh. Sure, Chris. Save your receipts and send them over after the trip."

I gave myself a big pat on the back. This was all too easy!

Then it hit me. Hard. "Oh, God," I thought to myself. I'd forgotten something. "I gotta get this past the MOM…damn."

After a week of intense bargaining, I managed to sell Carol on the idea of having Carissa go with me on yet another trip—all for the bargain price of giving up all rights to the next two Christmases and New Year's Eves. With our trip cleared and paid for, we were off.

We arrived a few days early, as I knew I still had part two of the plan to complete. I planned to sneak her into the men's professional event simply by showing up. By this time in her career, I had a pretty good understanding of how contests worked and I figured there was a good shot that some of the men wouldn't show up and there might be some open slots in the first-round heats. All I had to do was get her on the alternates list, so I searched out the event director to get the approval.

When I found him, it went something like this:

"Hi, my name is Chris, Carissa Moore's dad. We're here a few days early for the NSSA event and she wanted me to ask you if she could surf in the main event. You know, since she's just waiting around and all."

"Hmm. I'm sorry, but this is a men's event, and right now the event's full," was his reply.

I knew going into the conversation that this was a

men's-only deal, so I was prepared for my counter.

"How about if we put her on the alternates list and if there's no one else waiting around and a spot opens up, then she can surf? She said she'd love to go for a surf, just to get ready for the NSSA event. I mean, it's no big deal, but it would be great practice for her."

It worked. I'm not sure why. Perhaps it was my persistence. Perhaps it was because he figured there'd be no way a spot would possibly open up. Or maybe he just wanted me to leave him alone. But after he spent some time conferring with other contest officials and consulted the rulebook, which didn't say anything about a girl not being allowed to surf, he agreed. The gamble had paid off: she was on the alternates list.

Of course, I still I had to convince my daughter, which I knew would be no problem.

"Hey, Carissa! The event director came up to me and said there might be an opening in the contest! It'll be good practice for the main event, don't you think? You might as well; we're just sitting here. What do you think?"

Carissa was sold; besides, she trusted me.

"Really, I might get to surf today? OK, I'm in!"

Later that day, Carissa was given a spot in the contest. Almost miraculously, my plan had worked. I had made so much of an effort to get her into the event, and then was so surprised that she was able to compete, that I overlooked what we would do if she actually got in. Because she was an alternate, she would be surfing in less than half an hour. Our scramble to get ready began. As she suited up, I got her board out and did my customary check of her equipment. With less than ten minutes before the start of her heat, I discovered a big problem. To my horror, the fiberglass around one of the boxes that anchors the fins to the board was cracked. I had no time to prepare a backup board; we were staring possible disaster square in the face. The loose fin could break off at any moment. I realized now that this whole thing could easily blow up in our faces; if her fin falls off and she has no back-up board, she'll be out in the lineup unable to surf, and in an event where she's the only girl, this could be a monumental failure and it will be all on me. Her heat was about to start. There was nothing we could do, so I opted not to tell her about her faulty board.

"Go out and do your best," I told her on the beach. "Don't worry about anything. There's no pressure; it doesn't matter what you do here. You have nothing to lose."

As she walked down to the water's edge, I crossed my fingers that her board would hold up. The shoreline was blanketed by smooth, round, slippery cobblestones. She could slip and drop her board before she entered the water and it would be game over. I was now incredibly nervous. This whole thing could turn into a nightmare.

To add to the stress of the situation, the surf was onshore, chopped up by the wind and far from perfect. In the previous heats, most competitors had managed a turn or two with no real significant scores being posted. Oddly, Carissa had something going for her: by a twist of fate, she had Albee Layer in her heat, a boy she'd grown up surfing against in Hawaii. Whenever she had a heat with Albee back home, she always came out on top. Albee was her good-luck charm in that way.

Her three competitors jockeyed heavily for position to start the heat. No way were they going to give Carissa a clean look, as losing to a girl wasn't something that any male ultimately wants to do. All three caught waves, which put all of them down the point. This left Carissa all alone. Carissa paddled into a wave, but it immediately closed out. She was still out the back all alone, but her three competitors were quickly paddling toward her; she had about a minute before they'd be back in her zone trying to out-position themselves to get priority for the next wave.

A wave came. To be clear, the Wave of the Day came. She paddled into a nicely forming right-hander. Taking off, she seamlessly lined up the wave, channeling grace and style into each bottom turn and critical move, flawless transitions from maneuver to maneuver. Where every other wave that came through that day closed out, hers just kept lining up and allowing her to turn. It almost seemed like a dream sequence. She ended the sweetly mesmerizing performance with a forehand reverse. I had forgotten all about the defective fin. It was the best wave of the day.

I remember standing there in disbelief, watching her paddle back out. She'd not only risen to the challenge, but shattered any expectations I'd had. The judges threw her a perfect ten. A ten-point ride was the farthest thing from my mind before the heat started. Seeing a small contingent of Hawaiian surfers sitting on the shoreline cheering for her drove home what she'd just accomplished. It was unbelievable. A perfect ten—in her first professional men's surfing event.

23

At the U.S. Open, Carissa bounces back to make it through to the quarterfinals, but there's still a lingering feeling of uncertainty. There's an obvious lack of surf in the forecast for the remainder of the contest. We both know that in these situations luck has a huge hand in winning.

In the quarters, Carissa is up against South African Bianca Buitendag, the same girl who beat her in Rio. Carissa's pre-heat prep is good. She believes in her strategy as she runs down the beach to paddle out. Everything points to a successful heat. For the majority of the thirty minutes, Carissa does everything she can on the waves she catches. She surfs her waves well, successfully performing the two best moves of the heat, but the moves are performed as the wave shuts down. Quick rides often lead to low to average scores, and both rides score Carissa less than six points.

In a heat that has not allowed more than a single turn from either competitor, and with Bianca holding priority with only a few minutes to go, Carissa is vulnerable. In the dying seconds, our worst-case scenario comes true. Bianca finds a wave that allows her to link multiple turns. In the span of a few short seconds, she gets the score she needs and Carissa's lead vanishes.

The heat is over and so is our time in Huntington. The loss is a bitter pill to swallow. The lead in the world-tour rankings that we'd worked so hard to build at the start of the season is gone. Courtney Conlogue, who grew up surfing Huntington and is far and away the hometown favorite, places third and takes over the yellow jersey.

There's a new points leader in the world-title quest. It's a tough loss. I don't have an answer.

24

If there's a silver lining to our misstep in Huntington, it's that the next contest will take us to Lower Trestles. I feel very good about Lowers. It's somewhere Carissa's thrived.

Located in San Clemente, California, it's only forty miles south of Huntington, but it's a world away in almost every sense. Most importantly, it's home to one of Carissa's favorite waves. Lowers is located on the grounds of San Mateo State Park and is named after a wooden trestle bridge that surfers walk under to reach the beach. The park is tranquil, with unspoiled wetlands and a series of picturesque cobblestone points—a stark contrast from the hustle and bustle of the Orange and San Diego counties it intersects.

Specifically, the wave at Lowers offers a unique set of variables—variables that favor my daughter's brand of surfing. The wave breaks consistently almost year round, but loves a good south swell. It's become such an important wave on the international stage because it's easier to ride than most waves. Thanks to nearby San Mateo Creek, over the centuries the coast has evolved as a virtual playground for surfers. The unique bathymetry combined with thick offshore kelp beds helps keep the conditions clean on most days. In Huntington, the onshore winds chop up the waves; at Lowers, the kelp floating en masse on the surface just outside the break keeps the bump from gathering momentum. And unlike Huntington's ever-shifting sandbars, the waves at Lowers break over the rocks in the same spot every time. For a surfer, it's a million times more predictable and easier to read. Subsequently, these longer, smoother faces and well-shaped walls are conducive to high-performance surfing.

When Carissa was young, I made it a point to come here and surf. The wave at Lowers is fun, not scary, and whenever possible I wanted Carissa to have positive competition experiences when she was starting out. We'd hop on a plane to surf there a few times a year. In the early amateur years, the NSSA held its annual national championship at the coveted location each June. It was an ideal destination for the contest. For five years Carissa competed in the weeklong event and grew comfortable in this little corner of the world. Success here became a familiar friend.

In the days leading up to this year's contest, the Swatch Lowers Pro, Carissa's excitement is building. Again, she's been practicing well, and from what I can gather, she is confident and prepared. Of course, doubts always loom. She seemed ready at Cloudbreak and Huntington, but lost early. Carissa also knows that last year's event at Lowers was where she suffered her biggest mental breakdown, resulting in an early exit. Looking back at last year, the poor result was probably the biggest reason she lost the world title. She can't afford a repeat.

We take time to talk about the reasons behind what happened in the heats she's lost. We work on letting go of these fears and surfing this event with desire and passion. Recently we've been making a concerted effort to practice breathing exercises that are designed to help calm her body. The idea was that it would help Carissa get more into a relaxed mindset before heats, but as we've been doing more of it, I find it's really helping reduce *my* stress level. Breathing and talking positively is one thing, but I know that no matter how much she prepares and how hard she works, the outcome is never certain.

25

Carissa leaves for California a few days earlier than me. When I arrive, I find that she is settled in and happy. She looks relaxed and confident. Her warm-ups are good. She appears to be one of the in-form surfers in the water. Everything is in place for a standout performance. All she has to do is keep her demons from getting the better of her.

A four- to six-foot south swell arrives on the first day of the waiting period and the women are called up to surf in the afternoon in some of the best conditions Lowers has seen in years. Carissa has a field day and tears into wave after wave, running away with her first-round heat.

The waves aren't the only thing of interest in the heat. Carissa had surfed against thirteen-year-old Caroline Marks, from the East Coast. Caroline was a last-minute replacement; her injury not yet having healed, Stephanie Gilmore had pulled out just a few days before.

A big part of Carissa's career has been defined by her groundbreaking actions: the youngest to win an open national title, at age eleven; the youngest to surf in the Triple Crown, at twelve; the youngest to make a World Tour final, at fourteen; and the youngest to win a world title, at eighteen. For so many years, she has worn the label of the youngest to do this or that. Now she's on the other side of the equation, surfing against someone ten years her junior. It's a good indication of how quickly time has flown by.

It brings me back to when she was a fourteen-year-old and found herself surfing in her first World Championship Tour event, against seven-time world champ

Layne Beachley—who was more than twice Carissa's age. As the winner of the Roxy Pro trials at Snapper Rocks, Carissa was pitted against Layne in the very first round of the contest—certainly a daunting challenge for any young surfer.

Fortunately for Carissa, the surf at Snapper on this day was small and playful. I knew that Layne would have a huge advantage in experience, but because the conditions were so easy to read, Carissa would match up well. In fact, I thought Carissa might even have an edge. She was confident and comfortable, and most importantly I knew I could get her excited to compete.

I used Carissa's naïveté to her advantage. Because of her youth, she had yet to surf with the burden of expectation. I had a game plan for her that I thought would give her the best chance. All I had to do was convince her to surf without any fear of losing.

"Carissa, no one is expecting you to win. I know you love conditions like this, so go out and tear it up. I know you can win this thing!"

And then I said something completely unfathomable: "Look, she's old, she doesn't even surf that good. She's in trouble and she doesn't even know it!"

Carissa nodded her head. "Dad, you're right. I can do this!"

She ran down the beach, showed no concern or fear, caught waves, surfed them well, and won. Though Layne ended up advancing though the losers' bracket and setting up a rematch, the result was the same. Remarkably, Carissa had beaten the world champion twice in the same contest.

And she wasn't done. She continued advancing all the way to the finals before losing to another former world champion, Chelsea Hedges. In many ways, her runner-up finish at Snapper proved to me that she had what it took to compete for world titles in the years to come.

26

Soon she's into the quarterfinals, where she draws Tyler Wright, a two-time world title runner-up. It's a tough draw as Tyler has been one of the most dominant women in professional surfing over the last few years. She matches up well against Carissa. They share similar strengths in their surfing: both are powerful with deep arsenals of maneuvers to draw from. Their duels usually come down to clutch performances in the final minutes, which is absolute torture for me.

Their quarterfinal clash is no different. Fireworks start as soon as the horn blows. Tyler immediately paddles into a beautiful wave and lays down five critical moves in rapid succession. It's not what Carissa or I wanted to see. As much as I want to downplay the strength of Tyler's ride, I know a huge score is coming. As she paddles back out, the judges award her a near-perfect score: a daunting 9.93.

Tyler can now afford to be patient. She has twenty-five minutes to find just one more quality wave. Meanwhile, Carissa faces the formidable task of playing catch-up. She needs two excellent scores to get back in this. She has to get moving. She begins catching more waves and attempting maneuvers with a higher degree of difficulty in an effort to wow the judges.

Carissa's response to Tyler's score comes a few minutes later as she strokes into a medium-sized wave and surfs it well. She lacks the critical turns that Tyler had and the judges throw her a seven. She's on the board. It's still a big spread to cover, but at least she has something to work with. As Tyler waits for a good set wave, Carissa prowls the lineup looking for her next possible chance. I can only sit on the beach and find some solace in the fact that I can do nothing to influence the outcome. As much as I convince myself at times, I realize my psychic channeling won't direct the result of my daughter's heat. I sit on my little patch of sand and watch and wait—and stress.

As the clock counts down, I can't help but think to myself, "How can this string of bad results keep happening? What am I going to tell Carissa if she loses today?"

I think back to a year earlier, when Carissa had called me before her early-round exit from this event. She was unusually nervous. The pressure of defending her world title was evident. I was back on Oahu thinking that she'd be fine without me. I had miscalculated. The stress and pressure at that moment had gotten the better of her. I remember watching that heat on my computer. She surfed tentatively. Her usual brand of surfing was riddled with mistakes. I was beside myself because I could feel her losing composure and there was absolutely nothing I could do but witness her go through an emotionally tough loss.

This year is different. Her head is on straight. She is focused. She's done the work, done everything right. But she is still losing. I fear another bad result will be something she might not recover from. Tyler has been sitting for most of the last twenty-five minutes and by doing so has left the door open for Carissa. Both girls are holding onto small second scores with five minutes remaining on the clock. I know my daughter has a chance, but she'll have to make the very most out of her last opportunity.

With two minutes to go, a set looms. Carissa uses her priority and catches a wave that's lining up nicely but has a slight bit of chop on the face. She swings right. She pushes her turns as hard as she can to put together a series of strong forehand lip bashes and carves. Tyler is up next, but her wave breaks quickly and almost immediately shuts down, allowing her only one critical move. Time expires. The girls wait on the beach as the judges enter their tabulations. Carissa has to overcome a three-point deficit on her last ride.

Everything on the beach stops. Everyone is hanging on the judges' decision. It's a hugely pivotal moment in the season for us and the tension is palpable. After an agonizingly long delay, the scores are announced. Carissa earns an eight-point ride to Tyler's four. Her two-wave tally trumps Tyler's. Carissa wins! I don't know who is prouder—or more relieved. Carissa and I take a moment to celebrate. She cries.

Shortly thereafter, the contest is put on hold, and with a drop in swell in the forecast, the contest is called off for a few days. Carissa has time to regroup, rest, and refocus. She spends her down days catching up with friends and hanging out with her sister, who makes the trip down from Santa Barbara, where she is now attending college. It's a nice break after such an emotional quarterfinal victory.

Six days later, the final begins. For Carissa, nerves and stress seem to disappear. Good surfing is the result. Carissa has no specialty coaches for this event and I don't feel like I need to say too much before her heats. I convey to her a simple strategy: keep active in the lineup, be smart with wave selection, surf hard, and have fun.

Carissa sticks to the game plan. She surfs strongly and smartly enough to win the event and regain the yellow jersey. It's a huge deal for both of us. Last year Carissa lost the lead in the world-title race at this contest. This year she's re-established herself as the frontrunner. Her resolve to turn things around is a positive sign and I am tremendously proud of her.

27

With three events remaining, the pressure of winning a world title begins to intensify. Up until this point, Carissa has focused solely on surfing well in each event. There was no reason to get caught up in a world-title chase. The picture was clouded with too many different scenarios, but now, as the season winds down, spotlight begins to focus on the three surfers still in contention for this year's crown: my daughter, Courtney Conlogue, and Sally Fitzgibbons.

Carissa is currently on top of the leaderboard, but I am wary as we head into two European contests before the Tour takes us back home to Hawaii. We have travelled all over the world and surfed innumerable spots, but Portugal and France always feel especially foreign.

European surf challenges Carissa's approach and, consequently, my coaching. Huge tidal variances equate to a constantly morphing playing field. The ever-changing conditions make it extremely difficult to figure out what's happening in the lineup at any given moment. For a coach, the temperamental conditions make it hard to have a set heat strategy. In Hawaii, most of the reefbreaks undergo nominal changes with the ebb and flow of the tide, but the Old World boasts radical tidal shifts, up to twelve feet on some days. This drastically alters the surf. Lineups can move up or down the beach, out to sea, or onto the shore. It's all very much dependent on whether the water's flowing in or out. A peak Carissa might surf during her morning practice will have disappeared and resurfaced a hundred yards away by lunchtime. Add in swell direction, wave size, and prevailing winds and I've got a complicated stack of data to decipher before my daughter's next heat gets underway.

The first stop on our *tour de surf* takes us to Cascais, Portugal. It's a classic, old, cosmopolitan coastal town about a thirty-minute drive from Lisbon. On the way there, Carissa and I talk about how she's feeling.

"I feel good, Dad," she says. "I'm going to do this."

I believe her because I know right now she believes it, but I also know that despite the recent win in California and the championship crown hovering above her head, it's still not hers to claim. And being that we've been through this all before, I'm careful about letting complacency creep in. No matter how successful she is, there always seems to be something ready to throw her off balance.

The first challenge announces itself almost immediately after we touch down at the Lisbon Airport. Carissa's boards haven't shown up. It's a nightmare situation I've long been aware of, but have always had the fortune of not experiencing firsthand. Surfers, professional or not, swap horror stories of traveling halfway around the world only to land without their boards and equipment. For Tour pros in particular, traveling with surfboards becomes an exercise in patience. The bags are big, bulky, and cumbersome to lug around. Airlines respond to such inconvenience by charging fees—fees that are confusing, expensive, and totally arbitrary depending on whether your airline representative is having a good day or not.

The big board bags are essential. They obviously hold the surfboards, but they also serve as a catchall for other gear—fins, wax, leashes, and wetsuits. At cold-water locations, a wetsuit becomes as crucial as a surfboard. You can't surf without a board, and if the water has a bite, you can't surf for too long without a wetsuit. Complicating the matter for pros traveling on the 'CT is that wetsuits and boards are extremely difficult to replace. Professional surfers spend years fine-tuning specific surfboard shapes with their shaper. Custom wetsuits are the norm. Replacing either item is not as easy as going to a local surf shop and buying new ones. It's like Serena Williams replacing her tennis racket with one from Sports Authority the day before Wimbledon. It's doable, but far from ideal.

Our midnight arrival in Lisbon is already exhausting. The lost baggage only heightens the tension. After wasting an hour waiting in the oversize-baggage area, we make our way to another section of the airport in hopes of getting some answers. Are the boards still in California? Were they left behind in Munich during our layover? The airline representative, who doesn't look any older than my daughter, doesn't do much to actually locate the boards. The situation becomes a test in stress management. I employ the breathing and meditation exercises I was working on a month prior and manage not to lose my mind. It's a small, private victory, but I'll take it. Two grueling hours later, we leave the airport without the boards, but at least some measure of our sanity is still intact—until we get lost looking for our hotel.

Breathe. Focus. Repeat.

Carissa's lost boards are a serious issue. I'm looking down the barrel with only forty-eight hours before the contest is set to start and I do not want to think about the possibility of not having her equipment. I have a very limited window of time to either track down the boards or make preparations to find replacements. Both tasks are daunting, and to complicate matters, I don't speak Portuguese.

The next morning, I spring into action. I make calls to anyone I think may be able to help: Carissa's agent, our contact in Portugal, a Hurley team manager from France, the WSL Women's Tour manager. I notify everyone that she has lost her boards. Hell, I would have called Portugal's president if I'd had his number. I am vaguely aware some self-restraint may be helpful, but my temperament is to push rather than let things unfold. I become so singularly focused on remedying the situation that patience and diplomacy get shouldered aside in favor of a more aggressive approach. Somehow I feel justified in taking extreme measures. Carissa needs her boards.

Worse-case scenario, we still have one viable option. Prior to leaving for Portugal, I had Carissa swap a board with her friend and fellow Tour competitor Alessa Quizon. In theory she should at least have that one board to ride, but as luck would have it, it had been heavily damaged in transit. Just the same, a broken board is better than no board. I put a rush on the ding repair and hope for the best.

With the board challenge a work in progress, I turn to the wetsuit issue. The water in Cascais is frigid. Carissa needs her wetsuits. Buying or borrowing a wetsuit at this point is not an option. The damned board bag needs to be found! Agitated by the inadequate progress, I focus back on looking at how we can get some more help.

The contest's press conference is slated to begin in a few hours and I prod Carissa to talk about the situation.

"No matter what they ask you, bring the conversation around to dealing with your lost boards!" I tell her.

She assures me that she will mention it and then tells me to go for a walk, dismissing me from the press conference. She wants to handle things her way.

As much as I want the world to stop until she has her surfboards, it's ultimately Carissa's call, so I do what she requests and go for a walk. During the press conference she mentions her predicament far more gracefully than I would have. Her concern gets the attention of the contest director, who makes a personal call to the airlines. The next morning, the boards are delivered to the hotel along with her repaired broken board.

28

With the surfboards and gear found, we can now focus our efforts on the contest. Of the ten events on the Tour, Portugal is one of my least favorite because of the shortened waiting period—six days instead of the usual ten—and the site locations, which are less than stellar.

The Cascais Pro is a mobile event that features three separate surf breaks to choose from. Each day, contest officials confer and decide which break will be used. Though there are options, I'm still leery since the forecast models predict poor conditions throughout the entire waiting period. The models predict little to no swell at two of the locations, necessitating the contest director to utilize the remaining venue: Guincho Beach, a surf spot situated on a rugged and exposed section of Portuguese coastline.

Though Guincho will have swell, blustery weather is expected to accompany it. Our pre-comp practices are not fun. Back at home, we'd never surf in these conditions, but Carissa has no choice. She has to get in the water. Tidal fluctuations become a secondary problem as strong onshore winds churn up the waves into an almost unrecognizable form. I am beside myself.

My role is to analyze the conditions and then talk to Carissa about strategy—where to sit, which waves to look for, how to catch them—but the surf is so chaotic that I can't get any kind of read on what to do. I have nothing to give her. I find myself reverting to the kind of oversimplified suggestions I would give when she was six years old. *Paddle over there. Try to find a good one. Do some turns.*

To make matters worse, Guincho is a European mecca for windsurfing. Taking advantage of the robust winds, a pack of kitesurfers descends on the break. I watch helplessly as Carissa tries to find her spot amongst the fray. Surfing in the middle of so many people zipping in and out of the lineup is extraordinarily dangerous. It's hard for me to watch, let alone stay positive.

The event is put on hold for the first three days due to high winds. On the fourth day, things settle down enough for the event to get started. I'm relieved but not pleased. The surf is still lousy. There are instances where it offers a few well-shaped sections, but they're few and far between. Somehow Carissa finds a pair of scoring waves in her opening heat to advance. As the day progresses, the onshore winds get uglier and stronger and the contest is forced to go on hold until morning. I think to myself, "With these conditions, things can only get better."

I was wrong. We return the next morning to a sea of chaos. Instead of improving, the weather has further deteriorated. The ocean is dark and angry. Wave upon windswept wave churns itself into whitewater and hammers the shore. It's all very ominous, but the contest directors cannot afford to take another day off. With so little time remaining in the waiting period, heats are forced to run.

Reluctantly, I head down to the beach to confer. Once there, we face another delay: the dawn's low tide has made the waves almost impossible to ride. In cases where the event is put on hold, competitors take the opportunity to paddle out and practice, but because these conditions are so awful and the water so cold, it's a toss-up between paddling out and expending precious energy or just staying in and waiting. Carissa opts to stay warm. I concur.

By midmorning the tide fills in enough that heats can resume. Low scores are the order of the day. While it is usually advantageous for Carissa to watch other competitors surf before her heat, today it's pointless.

Though the tide is rising and the waves are becoming less dumpy, the onshore winds are intensifying, further whipping and chopping up the waves. Again the conditions go from bad to worse. Before Carissa paddles out, I search for some words of advice to give her. Though some of the smaller waves look good, I see no defined peaks and no set rhythm, either. My heart sinks; it's one of those rare scenarios where I have no proper strategy and thus nothing to say. She is on her own.

I watch as she tries to figure out the lineup from the water. It's a desperate situation; I'm lost on shore while she's lost at sea. For the better part of thirty minutes she struggles to find a wave that will allow her to do even one proper turn. I sit on the beach agonizing as the minutes tick down with no significant scores on the board. When the horn sounds, dismal reality sets in. There is no miracle comeback, no surf version of a Hail Mary. The heat was a disaster. In one fell swoop she loses her heat, the yellow leader's jersey, and, most concerning of all, her confidence.

29

The loss at Cascais is not what we need, but it's a sharp reminder that the ocean plays by its own rules. It wasn't too many years ago that Carissa and I traveled to the World Junior Surfing Championships in North Narrabeen, a suburb just outside of Sydney, Australia. At twelve years old, she was going to be competing against the best surfers under the age of twenty-one, and we knew it wasn't going to be easy. But we were both eager to gain some Aussie surf experience as we headed Down Under.

We arrived to playful surf with beautiful summertime weather. Though Carissa was the youngest in the field and untested in Australian beachbreaks, the conditions suited her. On the first day of competition, she advanced with relative ease. But the next morning a nasty disturbance blew in from the Tasmanian Sea and turned the playful peelers into wind-whipped chop. As the front hit, it brought strong onshore winds and heavy rain. The contest halted while the seas churned and water deluged from the sky. The petulant Australian seas were a far cry from our balmy island home.

Carissa was seeded into the first heat of the quarterfinals, which meant that she would be surfing in the very first heat of the day when competition resumed. She had to be ready each morning no matter what the weather. For a twelve-year-old used to sunny Hawaiian skies, just getting motivated to get out of bed each morning was a daunting task. To make matters worse, the onshore winds had also ushered in giant blue bottles—baseball-sized jellyfish with a nasty reputation for administering gnarly stings to anything that crosses their path. How could I possibly ask my daughter to paddle out in these conditions? It seemed outrageous and unacceptable. I wanted her to fare well in the contest, but her safety was certainly more important.

The wild weather continued for days until finally the inevitable came. An announcement was made over a lone loudspeaker outside the locked North Narrabeen Surf Club. Barely discernible over the wind's roar, it was decreed that the girls would get underway promptly at 8 a.m. Carissa would be competing in half an hour's time.

I was shocked, but we had no choice. We frantically got ready even though the event site appeared nowhere near ready to run. There were none of the usual tents or sponsor banners on the beach, no water safety, no contest organizers—no one except for a few equally confused surfers. We barely had time to get the contest jersey, let alone strategize. Carissa would be surfing completely unprepared. I was so off my game thanks to the weather, jellyfish, and last-minute announcement that I did a terrible job of giving her any pre-heat advice. And again it sounded eerily similar to advice given when I have nothing to give: *Paddle over there. Try to find a good one. Do some turns.*

Her heat was a disaster, packed with confusion and mistakes. How could she possibly be prepared for this madness? She was twelve years old. Carissa ended up losing, largely due to a priority mistake halfway through the heat. I was beside myself as she paddled back to shore.

"We traveled thousands of miles and spent ten days of our lives only to surf this crap?" I muttered under my breath as I made an abrupt turn and strode down the windswept beach, finally yelling my frustration into the roar of the wind.

"Fuck! Fuck! Fuuuck!"

I was sure Carissa couldn't hear me, and because the beach was empty, no one would see my building tantrum.

So I let loose a full-throttle, Category 5 Cyclone-level meltdown. It was ugly. Regaining my composure, I made my way to Carissa, consoling her on the loss as best I could. On our way back to the parking lot, a guy approached me. To my growing horror, I realized that he was a contest camera operator and had witnessed my entire tirade.

"That's no way to act, mate, You're gonna ruin your kid's career if you keep acting like that," he said with an Aussie accent.

He continued to lecture me as we made our way up to the car. Carissa listened wide-eyed and confused. I felt sick. Not only was the contest's outcome disappointing, but I was now fully ashamed of my own immature behavior.

Though I have similar feelings on Carissa's loss in Cascais, I know better than to stage a repeat performance. My humiliating experience at Narrabeen ensured it was a hard lesson learned.

30

After Carissa loses her heat in Portugal, we immediately leave. Neither of us feels like sticking around to see the rest of the contest. In fact, we actively try to ignore it so as to better nurse our wounds and clear our heads. We leave the contest area right away and head back to our flat, pack up our stuff, and head to the airport. Instead of flying straight to Hossegor, France, to prepare for the next contest, we hatch an escape plan: Operation Forget the Hell out of Surfing.

Though we don't want to think about the contest, it's killing us to know who won. On our way to the terminal, we decide that Luke should be the one to check the latest results. As it turns out, Courtney has won the contest and taken the lead in the world-title race. Anyone else would have been fine, but this result is really going to mess with Carissa's head. We have two weeks to regroup before the next competition, and getting out of surf mode will help set us straight.

At the airport, we discuss possible destinations. I approach the ticket counter and ask the agent if there are some reasonably priced flights available.

"When?" she asks.

"Today."

"Where?"

"Pretty much anywhere would be good."

As luck would have it, flights throughout Europe are either fully booked or prohibitively expensive, with one exception: Venice, Italy. The charm and beauty of Venice's waterways will ease the pain of Carissa's defeat. A new place, inspirational art and architecture, away from all things surf related, it should buoy her spirits.

The splendor of Venice is good for both of us. We get lost in the history and culture that is so far removed from our daily surf lives. After a few relaxing days, it's time to move on. We hop on a train to Salzburg, Austria, taking up an invitation from Red Bull to come visit their global headquarters. It's another much-needed distraction.

After a good night's sleep, we head over to Red Bull's on-site airport to visit Hangar 7. Designed and built for Dietrich Mateschitz, the founder of the company, it's full of toys. From airplanes to helicopters and Formula 1 racing cars, he's got it all.

Waiting for us outside, the Red Bull staff has an aerobatic helicopter warming up to give us a tour of Salzburg. I contemplate not going. I have a serious phobia when it comes to these kinds of things. When I was a kid, I'd get sick riding in the backseat of a car, and though I am much better now, the words "aerobatic helicopter" had me thinking twice.

"Come on, Dad, you gotta go. We have to do this," begs Carissa.

I don't need prodding. I have to go for it despite knowing what is in store. The next forty-five minutes is already scripted in my head: we'll start off with an easy flight featuring spectacular views, followed by a terrifyingly out-of-control white-knuckled helicopter ride and a severe bout of motion sickness.

Belted in, we lift off and head toward the architectural marvel that is Red Bull headquarters. We fly over pristine alpine lakes and enjoy viewing the countryside where *The Sound of Music* was filmed. Ascending over the top of a mountain, we hover thousands of feet above Salzburg. I know then it is time to pay the personal price.

The pilot points the helicopter straight down and we drop, and drop, and drop. Pulling out of the dive, we go into a series of upside-down turns and spirals. Again and again. After sixty seconds of complete terror, the pilot steadies the aircraft and a wave of nausea hits me.

"Is everyone OK?" he asks.

"Uh, no," I immediately reply.

As if on cue, he hands me a barf bag. I proceed to gag into it for the remainder of the flight.

Back on the ground, I know I'll need more than a few hours to settle down, so I hit the hotel to recover for the rest of the day. As I lie in my room, it dawns on me that this experience, strangely, is similar to my experience with Carissa on Tour. It's been an amazing ride infused with brief moments of fear and upset, but, of course, I wouldn't ever think of missing it.

31

The time off isn't all fun and games. There are moments when Carissa breaks down and cries over her loss in Cascais. I let her work through her emotions, but it's time to shift gears. The next event is right around the corner and she needs to get back into a good headspace. It's time to begin the rebuilding process.

I start by making sure Carissa knows that the caliber of her surfing is amazing right now. I inform her that with the end-of-the-year point adjustment, she is still leading the race for the title. I also tell her to stop acting like a baby, to get her shit together. In no way is she surprised at my directives.

All her life I've been able to get a sense of where she is mentally simply by looking into her eyes. It's easy enough for me to figure out if she's covering up something, if she's afraid, or if she's ready to take over the world just by the look she gives me. After our travels through Italy and Austria, I sense a renewed spark. The fire has returned to those big, beautiful brown eyes.

If only the surf were ready. In the days leading up to the Roxy Pro France, there isn't a wave to be found in Hossegor. Carissa makes the most of her additional time off by committing to beach workouts and checking in with friends, but she's antsy. She hasn't had a surf session she's been happy with since her win at Lowers three weeks ago. Our goal is to be as prepared as possible come the opening day of the event, but without waves to practice on, we're in a jam. We're going into this thing cold.

How I handle the downtime is no surprise. I'm

plunking away on the computer, studying forecast updates and climbing the walls. Waiting. Eventually the fruits of my agony reveal that a new swell is on the way.

The surf is due to arrive on the first day of the holding period. Great conditions are also on tap, and it should be all systems go. With two events left in the season, the importance of doing well becomes amplified. The pressure is on to get a result good enough to keep the title chase alive going into the final event, which will be held in Hawaii—our home turf.

There is a possibility that Courtney could win the world title if Carissa loses early. We don't talk about this scenario. I opt to not even tell her that it exists. I don't think she is even aware of it. Instead, I tell her that for this contest it's imperative she focus solely on each heat in front of her.

On the afternoon before the scheduled start, small waves begin to materialize. Forerunners of a new swell slowly fill in. Everyone takes advantage of the new pulse and Carissa welcomes the opportunity to get back on her board. I take my place on the sand and watch.

As I should probably expect by now, my after-practice critique takes an unusual turn. Carissa comes out of the water after her session and asks for feedback. I respond matter-of-factly, "The first half of the practice was great; you caught some of the better waves and surfed them well. But when some of the men paddled out, I thought you shied away from the better waves and settled for waves that didn't offer you the opportunity to surf as well."

There is no argument or excuse-making. No second-guessing my motives. Surprisingly, she simply nods in agreement.

"Yeah, I got intimidated when they came out. I need to get into the mix a little more," she says.

I crack a smile. Wow, a nonjudgmental response from my daughter. That only took twenty-three years! It appears we are making progress.

The next day—the first day of the waiting period—the surf is massive. The French coast is consumed by giant walls of whitewater. After a week of no surf at all, suddenly it's too big. The contest is called off because of the unruly conditions.

A day later, the ocean's calmed down and the heats begin. In an unlikely first-round pairing, Carissa faces off against Stephanie Gilmore. It's not often that a top seed will find herself going against the defending world champion so early in a contest, but because of her injury, Steph has dropped down the rankings. This matchup is not to be taken lightly. Steph is someone who could eliminate Carissa from the contest quite easily. As usual, I'm a nervous mess, but Carissa seems unfazed. She surfs well, and despite a solid showing by Steph, she wins the heat.

Carissa is fortunate to advance while upsets mix up the pairings heading into the quarterfinals. It ends up working in her favor, as Tyler Wright gets reseeded out of Carissa's bracket and into Courtney's. It sets up a critical fourth-round clash with some serious world-title implications.

With only two events remaining on the schedule, every result is now amplified. Carissa and I don't usually concern ourselves with what her rivals are doing, but now that the world title is within sight, results are hard to ignore. I spend free time crunching numbers and looking at world-title scenarios, but don't let Carissa in on it. Instead, I tell her to continue to block out what is going on around her, especially Courtney's heats, feeling it's better for her to focus on reading lineups and pushing herself to surf her best.

Regardless of what I am telling Carissa, I'm barely keeping it together during these critical match-ups. For me this is the worst kind of stress. I don't want to watch the heat. I just want to know who won. Instead of watching the clash between Courtney and Tyler, I go for a fitful beach run in an effort to exhaust my nervous energy.

Much to my relief, I return to the news that Courtney's lost. This gives Carissa a chance to regain the Tour rankings lead if she can get to the semis. Everything goes according to plan in the quarters, where Carissa surfs a great heat to advance. The world-title momentum has just swung back in her favor. Unfortunately, after that the contest is called for the day. The high tide has drowned the sandbar and the waves have stopped breaking. It's one of those curious circumstances in professional surfing: a contest can be called off in a moment's notice and everyone—fans, competitors, media, organizers—simply pack up and go home. Now we have to wait.

32

The final day of competition for the Roxy Pro is held on my birthday. For the most part, birthdays are just another day, but there is part of me that wants a victory for my present. I think to myself, "How great would it be to win here and all but clinch her third world title today?"

It's an extraordinarily cold morning for this time of year, cold enough for the condensation on our car window to freeze. It will once again be a challenge to deal with cold feet—good thing Carissa's boots are back in action and fully charged. A new swell has filled in overnight. The ocean displays a unique beauty this morning. The dawn wind blowing over the warmer ocean causes a fog to hang over the lineup. Though the beach is clear, the mist obscures the surfers only yards away. From what I can make out, Carissa looks good in her warm-up.

As the fog subsides, a right-hander in front of the contest area presents itself. The waves look fantastic and are letting surfers perform multiple turns. I'm stoked. Carissa's history is ripe with success in such conditions.

The contest starts promptly at 8 a.m. First up is the men's quarterfinals, which is followed by the women's semifinals. As the morning progresses, the ocean's mood begins to change. The first few heats start off with amazing surf, but as the tide drops, good waves become less frequent and the break slowly shows signs of decay.

I do some math in my head: Carissa will be up in a few hours, and by then the tide's going to be too low for the bank. By the time she surfs, the wave is going to shut down. "We're screwed," I think to myself.

Part of me wants to persuade the contest directors to put the event on hold for a few hours until the tide shifts back and the break reappears. It's not a farfetched thought, as this kind of thing happens from time to time. It's all part of competing in a fickle ocean. I opt not to partake in decision-making politics; instead I walk the beach and look for other possible areas that might be showing signs of life. With no obvious choice, I cross my fingers that the right-hander that has been working all morning will still be making some sense when Carissa hits the water.

We go over strategy. I suggest that she attempt to surf the right that competitors have been surfing all morning, but I also tell her she may have to improvise. I point out a peak down the beach that's showing some rideable faces. It'll be a big gamble. I am beside myself for the second time in as many contests. The ocean is changing and there isn't much I can do; Carissa is going to have to figure the lineup out as the heat unfolds.

It's not the first time last-minute changes have occurred. Two years ago, with the world title on the line, Carissa had to make a major strategy adjustment before her heat with Stephanie in Portugal. Steph had paddled over to another bank down the beach, and in a rare instance, I stood up and waved for Carissa to paddle down the beach to meet her. On that occasion things were successful. She won a close heat and the exchange played a pivotal role in clinching her second world title.

This time things are different. Though she quickly makes adjustments to meet her competitor down the beach, the waves are mostly closeouts. To make things trickier, a rip current is running through the break, pushing the girls out to sea. Carissa is confused for most of the heat and spends her time waiting for a wave that never comes.

It is eerily reminiscent of the loss in Portugal. Carissa's opportunity to gain more precious distance over Courtney has evaporated. To add insult to injury, she lost her semifinal with her lowest point total ever in her career: three points. On my birthday!

The next morning, we pack up our bags and head home. On the way we take stock of her position: though there were some tough losses, and despite the hardships and the tears, she's still in a great position to win her third world title. But, most importantly, she'll be able to make her stand in friendly waters.

33

After six weeks of highs and lows, I'm wiped out. Physically and mentally I'm drained, and Carissa must be doubly so. We talk about letting go of surfing on our flight home. We're in agreement: no surfing for a week. It's time to decompress—to forget about surfboards, wave riding, and competing for a while. I feel good about the decision. Breaks like this are important to recharge the batteries, and with six weeks until the final contest of the year, it's the best thing she can do. Our resolve is firm, and with these thoughts our mood is lightened and relaxed. We are coming home and taking a much-needed break.

We stay true to our script for all of twelve hours. Looking out the airplane window on our approach into the Honolulu airport, we watch clean corduroy lines march in toward our favorite reefs. The surf on the south side of Oahu is pumping. That is not normal for this time of year. By now this side of the island has usually entered its winter slumber, but a late-season swell is in full swing and the conditions are pristine. Is this a gift or a curse?

The thing about surfing is that you don't just stop. It's impossible to ignore good waves. They'll beckon back you back into the ocean every time. And surfers go to dramatic extremes to satisfy this impulse, from innocently calling in sick to work to more drastic measures like hopping on a plane and traveling halfway around the world to ride literally one wave. Right now the surf is as good as it gets in our little corner of the world, so hours after saying we're not going to dip a toe in the saltwater, our plans change. We're going surfing!

For me, that's the beauty of our sport. Forget the training and competition. There is an ingrained passion for doing what we do. Sometimes it's a job, but at its most basic, surfing is just plain fun, and when it's good it can be an almost spiritual experience. Jet lag and road weariness be damned: less than twenty-four hours after landing on Oahu, we've got our boards and are standing on the sand.

My only condition to getting back into the water so soon is that Carissa surfs simply for the joy of it, lets thoughts of wrangling a world title fall away for a few days. And she does just that. She's genuinely stoked after each session. After all these years, she still loves what she does. She loves to surf. That's all I could ever ask for.

Reinvigorated, she tells me she is ready to start planning for the last event of the season, the Target Maui Pro. There's a lot on the table, but she's looking forward to it. How could she not be? The event's location, Honolua Bay, located on the northwest corner of Maui, is not only one of the most pristine settings on the entire Valley Isle coastline, but is also home to one of the island's best waves—a perfect right-hand point that breaks off a reef and peels flawlessly for several hundred yards down into a turquoise bay. But, like a lot of spots, the wave's beauty is deceiving. It's nuanced. It will take Carissa hours of practice to reacquaint herself with the break's moods and to get a proper feel for the speed and pace of its sections. With this in mind, we decide on a training strategy in which we will fly over to Maui when a good swell presents itself.

Out of the water, I talk to Carissa about staying relaxed and positive. She has six weeks of downtime before the event begins. Her challenge will be to keep her focus away from constantly thinking about either winning or losing a world title.

On paper, I feel this contest favors Carissa's style of surfing more than any other wave on Tour. It features an easy-to-read takeoff zone, and it's a well-groomed right-hand wall with offshore winds. It's held at a location she has more experience with than the other girls. This is an event she should dominate. I don't know if this adds more or less pressure. This contest will be won by putting together a strong overall performance on the wave. It will take a display that includes powerful, well-timed turns and impeccable transitions between moves. In our practices I have Carissa commit to her rail game. She hones her big carves on the open face and ties them together with seamless bottom turns and fades.

I review forecast models daily. The combination of my weather-forecasting skills and our contacts' knowledge of which storms will push waves into the bay make our excursions to Maui an almost guaranteed success. In late October, two storms line up in the North Pacific. My goal is to make the trips as quick and easy as possible. Organizing the travel, boards, and accommodations is a bit of a challenge, but I make a game of it and see how quickly we can get from our house on Oahu to riding her first wave in the bay.

We take advantage of both swells. The first swell comes with a bit of a surprise; the surf is bigger than expected. After surfing smaller waves for much of the year, her first paddle-out comes with nervousness for both of us. When it's big here, the wave breaks with intimidating power. I had planned to film her sessions while on these trips, but with the surf being so challenging, I paddle out with her. For so many years I had been the one to look after her in bigger surf, so I still have that sense of duty when there's size. I want to be close to her in case she needs me. By now I realize my attendance in the lineup is more ceremonial than practical, and I spend the majority of the session on the inside watching from the channel.

In addition to heavy conditions, the lineup is tremendously crowded. Every surfer in Hawaii knows just how good this wave can get, and with the ease of predicting when a swell is due to arrive, surfers will make the drive—or, in our case, fly over—with the hopes of scoring one or two perfect Honolua peelers.

The intensity of the crowd gets me wondering if the effort is worth it. It can be frustrating making the effort in both time and expense and then getting so little actual surf time. Carissa has to be tactful in situations where she is not a regular in the lineup. Though people know that she is on Maui to practice for an upcoming competition, that doesn't dissuade them from taking a wave from her during one of the sessions. There are times when she doesn't catch a wave for thirty minutes. But there are moments when she finds some of the best waves of the session and surfs them well. It's those successful moments that I am proud of. It's difficult for a female to integrate herself into a male-dominated lineup and vie for the better waves. It's been something I've been working with her on over her entire career, and to see it come to fruition is tremendously gratifying.

Though her sessions on Maui are successful, back at home I notice she is becoming more and more tense as the contest nears. I feel for her. I can only imagine how difficult it must be to deal with waiting for a contest where she will either win a world title or fall just short. Being that this year has already had its share of ups and downs, I speculate that these feelings are compounded. I understand her enough to know just how much this world-title chase is beginning to consume her, and I do my best to keep her centered.

In the days leading up to the contest, Carissa has the opportunity to recommend the trialists for the Target Maui Pro. Target, which is also one of Carissa's sponsors, has asked her who she thinks should receive the wildcard into the contest. Carissa immediately picks her sister. She also throws the names of a few other rising Hawaiian stars in the hat, and after some discussion it's decided that there will be a four-person trials heat to decide who will get the wildcard. Now that I will have both daughters surfing in the contest, I immediately have to mentally shift gears.

After six weeks, the time is finally at hand. We fly over to Maui. I'm excited, as the forecast looks favorable. Boards are waxed and ready. We settle into our accommodations. Carissa's fit and happy. Everything's running smoothly.

Everything except that the predicted swell fails to materialize. Instead of well-sculpted right-handers rolling through the bay, it's flat. That's surfing for you, especially with a fickle mistress like Honolua Bay. While Honolua offers surfers a perfect wave, it also doles out its share of long flat spells. During these times it's better suited for swimming or snorkeling. The contest is forced to go on hold. The updated forecast indicates that it's going to be flat for almost a week. More waiting around means more time to think about the outcome. Carissa and I both become agitated. Thoughts of losing the title creep back into her head, and I'm bored. After I coax her back to a better frame of mind, I hop on a plane back home. It's for the best. My girls are safe on Maui and the current flat spell gives them time to reconnect.

On Thanksgiving I'm back on Maui to spend the holiday with, strangely enough, my ex-wife Carol's side of the family. I've heard the saying that time heals all wounds, and in our case that's certainly true. Carol and I not only get along but she's now one of Carissa's biggest fans.

It's a fitting time to give thanks to Carissa for having me continue to be a part of her journey. I tell her that regardless of the outcome of this world-title race, despite the craziness in Europe and the challenges with self-doubt in Fiji and California, win or lose, it has been a great ride this year.

I also remind her about her approach leading into last year's contest at Honolua. After she had fallen out of the title race, we decided to do something different. I told her that she should put less stress on her preparation and instead reconnect with the simple joys of going surfing. She surfed for the majority of her practices without any feedback and critique. I rarely went to the beach with her leading up to that last event. She surfed when and where she wanted, worked with her trainer when she wanted. I knew she had the skill set to surf the break at Honolua with very little preparation and that she understood the dynamics of the wave well enough. I wanted to take a chance on a completely different approach with the hopes that she would have a successful contest experience. She went on to win the event, and right now it serves as a good reminder of what happens when she's able to let go.

34

World Surf League cameras will be following Carissa through her warm-ups and pre-heat routines. Sponsor representatives and team managers have flown to Maui to support her for the event. Celebratory T-shirts and video clips are ready to be passed out as soon as she wins the title.

This might be my least favorite part of a world-title campaign: dealing with the pressures that come with being in the position to win it all. It adds more anxiety to an already high-stress situation. I know full well that Carissa's path to a world title includes traveling through this patch of expectation and scrutiny, so I do my best to block it out.

She has been through this scenario twice before and knows what to anticipate. Just the same, I do my best to deflect any unnecessary distractions from entering her psyche. There are "Carissa Moore 3X World Champion" T-shirts and hats hiding in my hotel-room closet. She certainly doesn't need to see them until the title really is hers.

In an effort to garner some space ahead of time, I take a moment to talk with the WSL commissioner about getting some reprieve from the cameras in the locker room. As much as I would like a place where she can hide from the attention, I understand their goal of capturing the drama. There's no getting around it; she's just going to have to deal with it.

On the first day of the contest, all my attention shifts to Cayla. Her trials heat is the first thing on the schedule and I get to paddle out with her and watch from the channel during the thirty-minute heat. Each competitor will be allowed to have a board caddy and I'll be taking on that role for her. (Because of the distance a surfer would have to travel in the middle of a heat to get a replacement board in case they lose or break theirs in competition, caddies hold onto a spare for them.) It is rare that surfers are allowed to have a caddy and I am tremendously happy to have the opportunity to escort her out to the break.

Cayla has a formidable task in front of her if she wants to advance to the main event. Her three challengers are more accomplished and experienced competitors. Plus, Cayla is a goofy-foot, which means her back will be facing the wave when surfing the right-handers rolling in at the bay. She's proficient in surfing in this stance, but it's not her strength.

Strategy-wise, I keep it simple. Cayla is to wait for set waves and then push her turns as best she can. She starts off with a few low-scoring rides before she finds herself out in the lineup with first priority. A beautiful set approaches. Cayla paddles into one of the bigger waves of the morning and navigates the drop perfectly. As she races the breaking section of the wave, she finds herself enveloped by the curl and pulls into a solid barrel section. I am simultaneously ecstatic and panicky as the wave swirls around her. She's not used to riding a wave like this, and the protective parent in me takes over.

I think to myself, "Go for it! Just, please, don't kill yourself!"

A few seconds later, the lip of the wave crashes into her head and she falls. As she tumbles underwater, I hold my breath. I know how dangerous a fall like this is; the combination of the wave's power and the awkwardness of her fall is concerning. But my fear is replaced with elation when she surfaces. She's smiling. She was thrilled with her ride and proud of her attempt. From that moment, I knew she would come away with a positive experience. Though she did not advance to the main event, it didn't matter. She had succeeded in my book. It was a very proud moment for both of us.

Before her first-round heat, Carissa is confident and comfortable, showing no signs of world-title pressures. I like how she is carrying herself. I think the excitement of seeing great waves eases the tension. It is six-foot and breaking with the most pristine, tropical conditions. It's picture-perfect out there. Carissa chooses the best waves, surfs them hard, and aces the heat. Both she and I couldn't be happier with the conditions and are excited that as the rounds progress the weather and swell holds. At the end of the day Carissa leaves the beach with two big heat wins. She's into the quarterfinals.

The next morning, the swell subsides and the bay is once again calm. We have two days before the next swell is expected to make landfall, so we go back into stress-management mode. To ease her tension, I update her on the world-title scenario: Carissa's advancement into the quarterfinals puts tremendous pressure on Courtney; she'll now have to win the event in order to amass enough points to surpass Carissa to claim the title.

I also tell her the irony that she may not have to set foot in the water to win the title. After losing on the first day of competition, Courtney still has to battle her way out of the losers' bracket to make it into the quarters. In order to do so, Courtney will face one of Carissa's longtime friends, fellow Hawaiian Coco Ho. Coco's dad and uncle are both former Pipeline Masters, and her brother, Mason, is an incredible free-surfer. She's even related to the late, great Don Ho. She's as Hawaiian as they come. She's a Tour veteran and I like her chances against Courtney in local waters.

A year ago, Carissa and Coco had an argument during a practice session at this event that left both of them a bit shaken. They've since reconciled and something tells me Coco's keen to stick it to the Californian. But before I get too carried away, I remind Carissa of our game plan: focus solely on her heats and do not watch Courtney's progress. There will be no resting in the Moore camp. Courtney's a determined adversary. She's not going to give up. It's going to be one hell of a finish, that's for sure.

35

It's finally here. Finals day. We wake up to a beautiful and clear morning. The swell has arrived and the waves in the bay are pulsing. The culmination of the year combined with perfect surf puts an electric charge in the air.

Our morning, however, gets off to a shaky start. In warm-ups, Carissa paddles out on a new board that doesn't respond in the way that she had hoped. Luke had paddled a backup board into the lineup, but after a few waves she decides that she doesn't like the feel of that board either. She comes in and starts to shuffle through her trusted boards.

"What's going on?" I ask her.

"Dad, I don't like either of these boards. I know I like this one, so I'm going to go back and catch a few waves with it," she responds.

I can tell she's frustrated. Her warm-up hasn't gone as planned and I'm getting the feeling she's having one of those moments. Extending her warm-up isn't the answer. It will only tire her out. It's an effort just to get to the lineup from where we are situated; she'll have to hike down the cliff, then paddle out and around the lineup just to catch a wave. With the lineup already saturated with surfers, it may take a while before she even catches a wave. Then she'll have to paddle back and hike up the cliff. That'll take at least thirty minutes. I don't see it as an option.

"Stop. You're not going back out. You realize you've already been out too long," I tell her.

"Dad, I am going back out," she sasses back. "I'm not ready."

Her anxiety is apparent. A moment of doubt has enveloped her.

"You've got this. You know you rip on that board. It'll take you another thirty minutes from here just to catch a wave; you're gonna tire yourself out. It's not gonna happen."

Despite my horrible delivery, Carissa sees some sense in my thought process. She pauses. Things settle down until Luke chimes in.

"If she wants to go back out, let her," he says.

My blood starts to boil.

"Luke has no damn business telling me what to do," I think to myself.

My ego's been hit, but this is no time for a family feud. Though I am stressing on the outcome, I am confident in her ability. The waves are good. She's healthy and focused. I know that there's no need to carry on with something as silly as this. We both know that regardless of her warm-up, she is ready. She has good boards, knows the lineup, and has been surfing impeccably. She just needs to control her nerves and let things fall into place. As for me, I need to settle down and not overthink things like warm-up protocol. The best thing I can do is let her do her thing. I am confident if she's in a good headspace a great result will follow.

Carissa has a few hours before her quarterfinal heat, so we drive back to the hotel to get a quick bite to eat and hide from the attention. It also gives us time to talk about things without people and cameras around. Any negative feelings from our morning squabble quickly fade away.

Settling in, Carissa puts on her headphones and listens to music. I spend the time pacing in the privacy of my hotel room. Waiting. Stressing. I assure myself that win or lose all this will soon be over.

We drive back to the bay about an hour before her heat, which just happens to be when Courtney and Coco begin theirs. The timing is by design. It prevents us from watching. Despite our attempts at ignoring the situation, on the drive back to the contest site the car is overflowing with tension. As much as I tell Carissa not to think about Courtney's heat, it's obvious that it's weighing heavily on her.

She then tells me something that gives me reassurance: "Dad, I don't want Courtney to hand me the world title. I want to earn it by winning the contest."

I drop Carissa off in front of the competitors' area before parking. This is also by design, as I've calculated that Courtney's heat is still in progress. In a similar exercise to Courtney's heat in Hossegor, I enact my latest ridiculous superstition: by not watching this heat, the outcome will somehow benefit Carissa. Besides, I'm freaking out. How wonderful would it be for this all to be over in a few minutes? I sit in the rental car and will the outcome to favor my daughter. I sit there fidgeting until I am sure the heat is over. It's an agonizing fifteen minutes before I exit to the sounds of cheers coming from the contest area. As I get closer I can see from the reaction from friends and family that Carissa has won her third professional surfing world title—while I was hiding in a rental car.

A wave of relief first washes over me. A season of incredibly hard work has just been realized. I know I should be celebrating, but instead I'm happy that it's finally over. Maybe I feel this way because this season has had so many ups and downs and was so emotionally taxing that finally knowing the outcome, especially a positive one, was like releasing a pressure valve that's been constricting my chest. I can finally breathe. I hurry over to the contest site to find Carissa. I find her amidst friends and family and I give her a huge congratulatory hug. I can sense her relief too.

And then I struggle with saying what comes to

mind: "So, how do you want to approach the rest of the event? The surf is firing. I'm thinking you want to win this one."

"I want to win the contest, Dad," she tells me.

It's not that I'm not satisfied. I am. For the most part, it's job done for the season. She's won. She's got nothing left to prove. It's just that right now the surf is firing and advancing means getting to surf longer at perfect Honolua Bay with no one out. That's motivation enough to put celebrating aside for a few more hours.

So it's back to business. I tell her she's going to have to quell her excitement and get back to focusing on her heats. Her quarterfinal is less than thirty minutes away. It's almost time to get her jersey and paddle out. With the surf this good, I can tell she wants to end the season with a bang. She's got that look in her eye. The waves are so much better than anything she normally competes in, and with the title sewn up, it is time to put the foot on the gas and see what she can do.

My job for the rest of the contest is simple: keep Carissa hydrated and focused amidst the mayhem. There is never much time between heats from the quarterfinals through to the finals, and with additional attention and interviews, there'll be even less. I do my best to cut interviews and fan requests short and make sure a cup of water is always at the ready. She's riding high. Almost before we know it, she's into the finals.

Finally it hits her. Carissa is starting to slow down from all of the action and excitement. But still her eyes burn with desire. I hand her one last cup of water and tell her how proud of her I am. Before she jumps into the water, she asks me for a prediction.

"Dad, what do you think it's going to take to win the finals?" she asks.

"I think someone's going to get a big barrel and win the contest," I smile.

Carissa's up against Sally Fitzgibbons, who has been surfing on point all contest. Sally finds herself in a similar position as Carissa was in last year. With nothing to lose, she has been surfing without the pressure of world-title expectations and it's been paying off.

Somehow the conditions and surf improve. It is all-time, classic Honolua when the girls paddle out. Carissa is in rhythm. For forty minutes she goes to an entirely new level. Her pièce de résistance comes in her selection of two beautiful waves that she dissects with the acumen of a neurosurgeon. The first hits the reef in the first few minutes of the heat. She takes off on a solid set wave and she whips off three massive, full-rail carves for a near-perfect score of 9.5. Her second comes about fifteen minutes later. She paddles into the biggest wave of the day and pulls straight into a beautiful barrel. She flies through the end bowl, accenting the ride with a high-lined grab-rail cutback to the delight of the crowd. A perfect ten!

"There you go, girl," I think to myself. "There's the barrel that wins the contest!"

I smile, knowing that at some point Carissa will say, "Dad, how did you know that was going to happen?"

The clock ticks down as I bask in her glory on the cliff overlooking the break. I am happy, beaming. I am as proud of this last heat as I am of the title. I have gotten everything I have asked for. In addition to winning the world title, she's won the contest with a near-perfect heat. Her top-scoring rides were two of the best waves I have ever seen her surf. In sport, it is so magical when an athlete performs on an almost unexpected level, and that was one of the rare times I have witnessed that from my daughter. I feel content knowing that on this day she is reaping the benefits of many years of hard work and dedication. The challenge for me was to help Carissa achieve something special, and this was one of those rare times where everything came together—the waves, the performance, and the victory.

The heat ends and the celebrations begin, plus everything that goes along with it: interviews, photographs, congratulations, high-fives, award presentations, champagne, and victory parties.

Carissa was greedy this year. She grabbed pretty much everything she could on this last day of women's surfing: the world title, the event, and the best wave of the year (it was confirmed at the WSL Awards Banquet in early 2017).

During the trophy presentation, I soak it all in. Sometimes, winning is a part of the journey I feel I don't enjoy as much as I should. I think it's because I like the challenge and the journey more than the final destination. As I watch Carissa hold her title trophies while being sprayed by champagne, I wonder if that is strange.

Today, however, I take more time to soak in the beauty of what she has accomplished. This is something we have worked for many years to achieve, and to have it pay off in the way that it has, and with a rare glimpse of perfection, I silently revel in her accomplishments.

36

What we want to happen is a far cry from what actually happens when we return home. Instead of decompressing quietly and taking a much-needed vacation as soon as we're back on Oahu, Carissa is inundated with a list of things to do: media requests, a five-day video shoot, the annual Surfer Poll awards. Unfortunately, Carissa is exhausted and wants nothing to do with any of it.

From an outsider's perspective I can see how this might seem strange—diva-ish, even. All of these activities are exciting and far from ordinary, certainly a world removed from the nine-to-five job that most people have. It's a difficult situation to grasp, but nine months of almost continuous stress and excitement has exacted a toll on her. Carissa needs a couple of days of doing nothing at all. I understand completely. I'm as exhausted as she is.

But as she's learned through her two previous titles, Carissa understands this is what comes with winning. She half-heartedly tackles her obligations as I half-heartedly help her manage her schedule. I have it easy. I don't need to act lively in interviews and functions. I don't even have to show up. So I don't. For the next ten days, Carissa takes care of the business end of winning the world title as I handle her affairs from a distance.

There is an item on her to-do list that is causing her anxiety: she's been invited to surf in an exhibition event at Pipeline that will run in conjunction with the Pipeline Masters. It's a big deal. It's an honor to get invited to perform at Pipe. The iconic break represents center stage in the surfing world. Each winter, traveling pros from around the world vie with local surfers for the coveted barrels on offer. The wave is as dangerous as it is perfect. Every wave is watched and every ride is scrutinized. It's a make-it-or-break-it wave. Literally one good ride can change a surfer's fortune. There's also an overabundance of testosterone floating around the beach.

Over the past few weeks several of her friends have been hurt. One suffered a major concussion, another shattered his pelvis, while another drowned and had to be resuscitated by a fellow surfer.

"I'm scared, Dad, but it's something I need to overcome," confides Carissa one afternoon.

"I understand. It's your decision. You don't have to surf if you don't want to. And if you're not feeling comfortable or confident, don't do it; that's how people get hurt out there," I say.

I've been taking Carissa to Pipeline for years, usually on smaller or less-than-perfect days. It is the one place I've felt I couldn't force her to surf. Though she's had the talent to surf the wave properly for a while now, it's taken years for her to become comfortable in the lineup.

This particular event will be held in conjunction with the men's Pipeline Masters, and there's a good chance the waves will be big. She realizes that with all of the stress of winning the title, she may not be in the right headspace. I give her my blessing that it's OK not to participate.

"You've proven yourself enough this year. If you don't want to do it, don't do it," I continue.

Truth be told, there's a part of me that wants her to do well here. The event will be watched and it's a way for her to cement herself as one of the best. She has the ability to surf the wave properly, and the idea of surfing empty Pipe keeps her from pulling out forthright. I suggest that she wait until the actual day of the event before making her decision, and she concurs.

"Who knows? It could be your best chance all

winter to get a good one out there," I say.

Regardless of her fears, the challenge of surfing a perfect barrel is too enticing to pass up. Carissa heeds my advice and keeps her spot on the roster. Plus, she knows that the event will be purely for fun—no points or world-title implications, just surfing for surfing's sake.

In the days leading up to the exhibition she wavers from one side to the other on whether to surf the event or not. I leave the decision making up to her. I've stressed outcomes enough this year. This one is completely up to her.

A few days into the holding period, I get a call. "Dad, I'm going to surf the event. It looks pretty fun right now," she says.

"What? You're on the North Shore? When will you be surfing?"

I'm caught off guard by her change of attitude. I was half expecting her to pull out of the contest, but instead, without telling me, she's driven across the island and is getting ready for her heat.

"They're thinking of putting the men on hold, then sending us out around lunchtime," she says.

I jump in the car and speed out to the North Shore. When I arrive at the house that her sponsor, Target, is renting for her for the winter, she's setting up her boards and talking to Pancho Sullivan about where to sit and which waves to look for. I'm pleasantly surprised as I realize she's taken it upon herself to prepare for this and that she's serious about it. There's still a part of me that wants to be part of the action, so I grab a board and start waxing it.

"Dad, it's good. I already did that," she tells me.

"OK. You want to talk about strategy?"

"I've been watching and I've talked it over with Pancho. I'm just going to wait for a few waves that line up on the rights."

"Want me to walk down with you?"

"No. Just cruise here, I'll be fine."

That part of me that is so used to being involved in decision making and supporting her is left wondering what to do now. After all we've been through, I've just been brushed aside. I guess she doesn't need her dad anymore I think to myself. But after a quick ego check, I know that this is the absolute best thing for her: to take matters into her own hands. It has to be done. It's all part of the process.

With nothing to do, I post up on the porch and settle in for her heat. I feel good. I'm not nervous or anxious. Maybe it's easier because I know the outcome of the year is already decided and the heat doesn't carry any real significance. Maybe it's because the surf doesn't look all that intimidating; after all, they've called off the men for the day because of the conditions. I'm realistic. Odds are Carissa won't find much out there today. There simply isn't much on offer.

She paddles out alongside title runner-up Courtney, rookie of the year Tatiana Weston-Webb, and ex-Tour surfer and big-wave charger Keala Kennelly. As the heat begins, Carissa watches as her competitors all catch waves. Carissa sticks to her game plan and waits out the back.

Midway through the heat, an A-frame peak angles in from just the right northerly direction. It's a perfect wedge for a Backdoor Pipeline barrel. But there's a slight problem: Carissa's sitting a little too far inside and has to paddle out to meet the wave before spinning around and catching it. Swinging around and making the drop from under the lip is far from ideal. The wave comes in quickly before it is slowed by the drag of the shallow reef. The crest of the wave lurches forward, creating a beautiful yet extremely dangerous barreling section.

Carissa knows what she has to do, and she knows she has to do it quickly. Any hesitation and she'll be done for. She spins around at just the right time, strokes as hard as she can, and rises to her feet as the wave begins to pitch out. She draws a flawless line, successfully driving through the swirling maelstrom.

It's one of those moments that's taken years of practice and is over in the blink of an eye. It's an effortless performance. I'm blown away. I know how difficult it is to ride the wave, and though it's something we've worked on, I know it is something I could never make her do. This comes from a desire from deep within. It is simply beautiful.

And she isn't done. A few minutes later, another opportunity arrives. She is now far enough out to set up properly for one more incredible barrel ride. This time she is able to paddle in early and stand straight up in the best barrel she's ever had at Backdoor Pipeline. As she rides out stylishly with the spray, it is a magic moment for both of us. As the heat ends, I have a smile plastered across my face from ear to ear.

Epilogue

I got lucky. I wrote this book as each event unfolded during the 2015 season, and things could have gone so many different ways. Though she had won two world titles, there was no guarantee she would win a third. I questioned myself as to whether I should be writing in this fashion. *What if she doesn't win?*

I knew my intention for writing this story was never about coaching Carissa to be the best surfer in the world; instead, it was about the journey. I wanted to write in a way that shared my feelings while navigating such a path, even at the expense of sounding ridiculous at times.

My actions are unique to who I am. I will always get nervous during events that matter. I will get impatient waiting through down days. I still enjoy the feeling of winning and abhor the feeling of losing. Armed with what I knew about myself and understanding that my driving motivation has always been to do what I feel is best for my children, I simply tried my best.

I am not an expert. My experiences are just that: experiences. I wanted to describe events and feelings in a way that any parent going through their own personal journey with their children might relate to. Learn from my successes and avoid my failures. Life's a journey. Keep your heart in the right place and embrace every second of it.

Acknowledgements

I would like to say a very heartfelt thank you to everyone that was involved in this book and Carissa's career. I'd like to start by thanking my ex-wife, Carol. It hasn't always been easy, but together we've raised two beautiful, dynamic young women who couldn't make us any more proud than they already do. When it comes to managing Carissa's career, a huge amount of gratitude is due to my mother, whose unwavering support and diligence in keeping her financial affairs in order has been invaluable. Love you, Mom! To Carissa's agent, Bryan Taylor, thank you for always standing by Carissa and your invaluable council over the years. Thanks Matt Biolis and Tom Nesbit for all the amazing surfboards over the years. Thanks to coaches Myles Padaca, Pancho Sullivan, Davey Gonsalves, Shane Beschen, Trevor Hendy, Andrew Sheridan, Cahill Bell-Warren, Adam Robertson, Wayne Bartholemew, Pat O'Connell, Brandon Guilmette, Mitchel Ross and Philippe Malvaux for their support and guidance around the world. To Carissa's sponsors, especially Red Bull, Hurley, Nike, Target and Roxy, your support has made so much of this possible. To the NSSA, especially Bobbi, Miko and Janice, thank you for providing Carissa and so many other kids with a platform to learn and excel. Thanks to the WSL for creating a tremendous world-wide stage for the girls to perform. Thanks to all of her competitors, both male and female, that pushed her to be her best. And a big mahalo to all the surfers in Hawaii and around the globe that have made my daughter's journey a positive one. A special thank you to Kim Stravers for copy editing and her input in the final stages. And to RF.

Christopher Moore

Chris was born in Honolulu and took to the ocean almost immediately. He swam competitively throughout his childhood, most significantly contributing to two Western Athletic Championship swimming titles for the University of Hawaii. After college Chris competed in national and international ocean races. Chris never surfed competitively, but his passion for the sport has led to an intimate understanding of the ocean around the islands. He attributes his background in swimming and love for the ocean to being the cornerstone of his success in coaching his children. First Priority is his first book.

Jake Howard

Jake Howard grew up surfing and exploring the Northern California coast. After a stint playing water polo in college at the University of Massachusetts, he left the cold East Coast behind and began lifeguarding in the Southern California beach town of Seal Beach, where he also began writing. For the past 15-plus years he's covered the sport of surfing and written for The Surfer's Journal, ESPN, Surfline.com, Surfer Magazine, as well as numerous international publications. He currently lives in San Clemente, California, with his wife and daughter.

Made in the USA
Coppell, TX
06 November 2020

40882003R00083